Acing

Intellectual Property

A Checklist Approach to Solving Intellectual Property Problems

W. Keith Robinson
Co-Director of the Tsai Center for Law, Science and Innovation
Altshuler Distinguished Teaching Professor
and Associate Professor of Law
Southern Methodist University Dedman School of Law

Series Editor
A. Benjamin Spencer

ACING SERIES®

Acing Series is a trademark registered in the U.S. Patent and Trademark Office.

© 2018 LEG, Inc. d/b/a West Academic
    444 Cedar Street, Suite 700
    St. Paul, MN 55101
    1-877-888-1330

West, West Academic Publishing, and West Academic are trademarks of West Publishing Corporation, used under license.

Printed in the United States of America

ISBN: 978-1-63460-273-0

This book is dedicated to Dylan and Sydney.

Introduction

The typical Intellectual Property ("IP") survey course in law school covers four subject areas. As a result, IP study aids can be lengthy and intimidating. In contrast, this book focuses on the core IP survey concepts. It organizes the most commonly tested IP topics in a way that will allow students to strategically approach IP problems.

A student's experience in an IP survey course can vary. Generally, IP survey courses are three to five credit hours. They cover subject areas including trademark law, patent law, copyright law, and trade secret law. Law schools often offer any one of these subjects, if not all, as their own course. Time restraints force instructors to make difficult decisions about the depth of coverage. Thus, the IP survey course poses an interesting challenge for instructors and students.

This challenge is compounded by another factor. IP scares some students because "it's what the engineers in law school study." In my experience, the students who perform best on my exams do not have a technical background. Instead, they have a good understanding of the legal issues in all four IP areas. This enables students to analyze IP problems with precision and clarity.

This book provides you with tools to do the same. It summarizes topics in the areas of patent, trademark, copyright and trade secret law. Each chapter will include (1) a Review of the topic, (2) a Checklist, (3) Problems and (4) a Points to Remember section.

The Review section is a student-friendly summary of the fundamental rules. The Review attempts to distill each area down to its essentials. Students who master these essentials position themselves to have success on their final exam.

After the Review, this book features a Checklist as a key analytical tool. The Checklist should not substitute for your course outline. Instead, the Checklists provide students with a clear roadmap to answer IP questions. Students should use the Checklist as they work through IP problems and to make their course outline more useful on the exam.

Following the Checklist, each chapter includes Problems. The Problems assist students in applying the various legal doctrines to fact patterns presented on a typical exam. The book provides brief answers to the problems so that students can check their work. Students who use the checklist approach can produce accurate and well-analyzed exam answers. Finally, each Chapter ends with Points to Remember that recap important issues.

This book is not intended to be a comprehensive treatise or study aid for all intellectual property issues. Since coverage in IP courses varies, this book focuses on the core issues in each subject area. I have observed that students that master these concepts consistently outperform their peers on the exam. Thus, this book attempts to aid in the reader's understanding of IP's essential tenets.

Writing this book has been a long process. I am indebted to my research assistant, Josh Smith, for his diligent work. I am thankful to my wife, Ty, for her support and to my two beautiful children for never letting me take things too seriously. My sister, Dr. Lakesha Goff, pushed me toward the finish line. Finally, I must thank my parents, Doris and Walter Robinson who taught me the value of education and hard work.

W. KEITH ROBINSON

December 1, 2017

About the Author

W. Keith Robinson is the Co-Director of the Tsai Center for Law, Science and Innovation and an Associate Professor at Southern Methodist University ("SMU") Dedman School of Law. Professor Robinson has taught intellectual property law courses for eight years, beginning as an adjunct at George Washington University Law School and currently at SMU Dedman School of Law. In 2017, Professor Robinson won the SMU Altshuler Distinguished Teaching Professor Award. In addition to teaching the intellectual property survey course, Professor Robinson teaches property and an advanced intellectual property course.

Professor Robinson is a graduate of Duke University School of Law (J.D., *cum laude*, 2004). He holds a degree in electrical engineering from the Duke University Pratt School of Engineering (B.S.E. 1999). Upon graduation from law school, Professor Robinson practiced law at Foley and Lardner LLP in Washington, D.C. He joined the law school faculty at the SMU Dedman School of Law in 2011. Professor Robinson is admitted to practice law in the District of Columbia, Virginia, and before the U.S. Patent and Trademark Office.

Table of Contents

Acing

Intellectual Property

A Checklist Approach to Solving
Intellectual Property Problems

CHAPTER 1

Trademark Subject Matter

A broad range of subject matter may be eligible for trademark protection. Any word, name, symbol, or device that identifies or distinguishes a source of goods or services can become a valid trademark. In addition, there are different categories of marks: trademarks, service marks, certification marks, and collective marks. These marks serve different purposes for both their owners and the public.

Typical IP survey exam questions will include issues concerning acquiring and enforcing trademark rights. Thus, students must understand what subject matter can be protected under trademark law. Chapter 1 summarizes the legal rules needed to address most trademark subject matter issues raised on an IP exam.

TRADEMARK SUBJECT MATTER REVIEW

Trademarks

Researchers have found unique markings on ancient artifacts such as pottery, bricks, and paper. These ancient markings served several purposes including to identify the person or persons that made the item. The markings also were an indicator of the quality of the work and a way for craftsmen to advertise their goods and services. Trademarks serve similar purposes today.

Any word, name, symbol, device, or combination thereof which is used to identify or distinguish a source of goods can become a valid trademark. Legal protection of trademarks preserves the integrity of the marketplace for consumers. In turn, this reduces consumers' costs related to making purchases.

The law governing trademarks is a combination of common law and federal law. Most IP survey courses will focus on the federal law as detailed in the Lanham Act. While federal law does not create a trademark, the Lanham Act does serve several purposes. First, it allows a trademark that is being used in commerce to be registered on the principal register. Second, once registered, the Lanham Act provides legal benefits that help protect trademark owners against misappropriation of their marks.[1]

The Lanham Act defines the term "trademark" as any word, name, symbol or device, or any combination thereof used or which a person has a bona fide intention to use in commerce to identify and distinguish her goods or indicate the source of goods.[2] For example, the word EXXON is used to distinguish the producer of petroleum products.[3] The Lanham Act also defines more categories of marks that may be registrable and entitled to protection including, service mark, certification mark, collective mark and trade name. The next three sections discuss these categories in detail.

Service Marks

Service marks identify and distinguish the services of its owner. It includes any word, name, symbol, or device or combination thereof. Examples of qualifying services may include providing music lessons or tax preparation. Also, applicants can register character names and features of entertainment programs as service marks. Despite these differences, both service marks and trademarks are subject to similar legal standards.[4]

Nontraditional Trademarks

In addition to words or symbols, the law recognizes rights in nontraditional marks. Sounds, smells, texture, motion, and color are eligible for trademark protection.[5] For example, the National Broadcasting Company (NBC) has a trademark on the three chimes played in association with its television broadcast. A court has found that the fragrance emitted by sewing thread is also protectable under trademark law. The Supreme Court has also held that the law does not preclude color from being a protectable trademark.[6]

Like other marks, the law imposes certain requirements on nontraditional marks. A nontraditional mark is eligible for protection if it identifies a source of goods or services. But, with the exception of sound marks, the USPTO will only register nontraditional marks

---

[1] Matal v. Tam, 137 S. Ct. 1744, 1752 (2017)("This system of federal registration helps to ensure that trademarks are fully protected and supports the free flow of commerce.").

[2] 15 U.S.C. § 1127.

[3] 1–1 Gilson on Trademarks § 1.02[1][b] (2017).

[4] Gilbert/Robinson, Inc. v. Carrie Beverage-Missouri, Inc., 989 F.2d 985, 988 n.1, 26 U.S.P.Q.2d 1378 (8th Cir. 1993) ("Trademark law treats trademarks and service marks the same.") *abrogated on other grounds by* Lexmark Intern., Inc. v. Static Control Components, Inc., 134 S.Ct. 1377 (2014).

[5] 1–2 Gilson on Trademarks § 2.11 (2017).

[6] Qualitex Co. v. Jacobson Prod. Co., 514 U.S. 159 (1995).

that have acquired secondary meaning. Secondary meaning is discussed in detail later in this chapter.

Certification Marks

Like trademarks, a certification mark can be any word, name, symbol, or device. But, certification marks differ from trademarks and service marks in two important ways. First, a certification mark notifies consumers of (1) origin, (2) characteristics or (3) that labor on the good or service was performed by members of an organization.[7] Second, a certification mark is not used by its owner.

Instead, certification marks are used by parties that produce a good or service as specified by the mark owner. For example, the mark COGNAC indicates the geographic origin of brandy—Cognac, France. The mark VERIFIED NON-GMO (genetically modified organism) signals a quality about food. Finally, CFL (Certified Financial Litigators) verifies that the service provider has completed a CFL course.[8]

Collective Marks

Collective marks are used by a member of an organization to denote membership or affiliation with that organization[9]. Collective marks also identify the goods and services of the members of the organization. The owner of the mark establishes the requirements for use and controls how its members use the mark[10]. The Atlantic Coast Conference (ACC) logo is an example of a collective mark. The colleges and universities that are members of the ACC can use this mark in association with their goods and services.

Trade Dress

Trade dress protects the overall appearance of a product (the product design) or a product's packaging. Trade dress is an expansion in scope in what the law traditionally recognized as trademark subject matter.

The two common issues that arise concerning trade dress are (1) determining what subject matter is eligible for trade dress protection and (2) understanding how the functionality doctrine places limitations on what packaging and designs are eligible for protection.[11] The legal standard for trade dress differs depending upon whether subject matter is considered a product design or

---

[7] 15 U.S.C.S. § 1127.

[8] 1–1 Gilson on Trademarks § 1.02[5][b] (2017).

[9] 15 U.S.C.S. § 1127.

[10] 1–1 Gilson on Trademarks § 1.02 (2017).

[11] The functionality doctrine is discussed later in this chapter.

product packaging. Therefore, it is important to distinguish between product design and product packaging.

Product Packaging

Product packaging includes any elements used in packaging or presenting a product to a consumer.[12] Product packaging is seen as a source identifier and is therefore capable of being inherently distinctive. For example, the Supreme Court held in *Two Pesos, Inc. v. Taco Cabana, Inc.*, 505 U.S. 763 (1992), that the decor of a Mexican themed restaurant (akin to product packaging) was inherently distinctive and therefore protectable trade dress.

Product Design

In contrast, a person seeking to protect a product design under trade dress must show that the design has obtained secondary meaning. In *Wal-Mart Stores, Inc. v. Samara Bros., Inc.* 529 U.S. 205 (2000), the Supreme Court explained that product design cannot identify the source of goods and held that to be projectable as trade dress, the product design of a child's dress had to have acquired secondary meaning.

What if a particular item, e.g., a Coca-Cola glass bottle, is considered both product design and product packaging? Generally, the law characterizes these items as product design. The consequence of this characterization is that to be protectable, the owner must demonstrate that the product design in question has acquired secondary meaning.

Trade Names

A trade name is any name used by a person to identify a business or vocation.[13] Unless a trade name is used as a trademark (identifies the source of a good or service) a party cannot register a trade name under federal law.[14] But, trade names can be protected under common law, and may be registered under state trademark law. In most states, the Secretary of State's office is responsible for registering and recording trade names. The owner of a trade name has permission to use the trade name in association with their particular business.

Distinctiveness

The law organizes potential trademark subject matter along a spectrum of distinctiveness. A mark's distinctiveness affects whether

---

[12] 1–2A Gilson on Trademarks § 2A.02[3] (2017).

[13] 15 U.S.C. § 1127.

[14] 1–1 Gilson on Trademarks § 1.02[6] (2017).

it is protectable as a trademark. On one end of the distinctiveness spectrum, there are generic marks. On the other end of the distinctiveness spectrum, there are arbitrary or fanciful marks. Descriptive and suggestive marks fall in the middle.

As shown below, subject matter can be characterized into one of the four categories along the distinctiveness spectrum. Where a mark falls on this spectrum can be determinative of what legal standards are applied to assess a mark's strength. It can also impact the outcome of a trademark infringement suit.

Trademark Distinctiveness Spectrum

Category	Generic	Descriptive	Suggestive	Arbitrary or Fanciful
Eligible for trademark protection?	No.	Maybe. Protectable if acquired secondary meaning.	Yes. Inherently distinctive. Protectable and no secondary meaning required.	Yes. Inherently distinctive. Protectable and no secondary meaning required.

Inherently Distinctive Marks

Inherently distinctive marks lie on the most protectable end of the distinctiveness spectrum. Subject matter is inherently distinctive if it intrinsically serves to identify a source of goods or services.[15] Inherently distinctive marks are automatically eligible for trademark protection. Evidence that the mark has secondary meaning is unnecessary. There are three types of inherently distinctive marks—(1) suggestive marks, (2) arbitrary marks, and (3) fanciful marks.

Suggestive Marks

Suggestive marks require imagination to associate the mark with the good or service. An example of a suggestive mark is Chicken of the Sea. Chicken of the Sea is a brand of tuna. The term Chicken of the Sea may suggest that the tuna is plentiful, nutritious, and similar to chicken, that the taste is agreeable to most people.

---

[15] Two Pesos, Inc. v. Taco Cabana, Inc., 505 U.S. 763, 768, 112 S. Ct. 2753, 120 L. Ed. 2d 615 (1992).

Arbitrary Marks

An arbitrary mark makes use of a common word that does not describe the associated good or service. The word mark "Apple" used in association with computers is arbitrary. The word apple is a name for a fruit. However, it is unexpected to associate a fruit with computers and related technology. Therefore, the way in which the common term apple is used makes it an arbitrary mark.

Fanciful Marks

A fanciful mark is an invented word or phrase that has no dictionary meaning at all. Kodak is an example of a fanciful mark. Kodak is a brand that we associate with photographic film, cameras, and other photography related products. Kodak is a fanciful name for a company that sells camera products because there is no relationship or association between the word Kodak and camera film other than to denote Eastman Kodak Company as the source of the goods.

Inherently Distinctive vs. Descriptive Marks

Whether a mark is suggestive, arbitrary or fanciful does not have as much legal significance as the distinction between inherently distinctive marks and descriptive marks. The outcome of a trademark infringement suit may depend upon whether a mark is characterized as inherently distinctive or descriptive because descriptive trademarks require secondary meaning. The next section discusses descriptive marks and secondary meaning.

Marks That Require Secondary Meaning (Descriptive Terms)

Subject matter that is not inherently distinctive may still be protectable as a trademark. Examples include descriptive terms, geographically descriptive terms, personal names and nontraditional trademarks such as colors.[16] This chapter has already discussed nontraditional trademarks and will address geographic terms and personal names in the section titled Limitations on Trademark Subject Matter. This section focuses on descriptive terms.

A term is descriptive if it immediately conveys a feature, characteristic, ingredient or function of goods or services.[17] For example, the mark "BRIGHT" could be merely descriptive of a lightbulb, and the mark "WET" could be merely descriptive for a car wash. These marks are considered merely descriptive because their

---

[16] 1–2 Gilson on Trademarks § 2.09 (2017).

[17] Anheuser-Busch, Inc. v. Holt, 2009 TTAB LEXIS 599, *13, 92 U.S.P.Q.2D (BNA) 1101, 1105, 92 U.S.P.Q.2D (BNA) 1101 (Trademark Trial & App. Bd. Sept. 16, 2009).

primary meaning does not identify and distinguish the source of the associated products or services.

Several tests exist for determining whether a term is descriptive.[18] First, a court may use the dictionary as evidence of the ordinary meaning of the term in question. Second, a court may apply the imagination test. Suggestive terms require a consumer's imagination to determine a product's characteristics. In contrast, descriptive terms convey product characteristics. The third test assesses a competitor's need to use terms in a trademark in describing their product. Typically, descriptive terms will be useful to competitors in describing the product. Finally, the fourth test examines the extent of the use of the term by others on similar products. A term is likely descriptive when several parties use it to describe similar products.

If a mark is descriptive, then to be eligible for trademark protection the law requires that the mark have secondary meaning. A mark has obtained secondary meaning when the consuming public associates the subject mark with a particular product or a specific source of goods.

Several nontraditional marks (defined *supra*) are considered descriptive and therefore require secondary meaning. In *Qualitex*, the Supreme Court held that the law does not preclude color from being a protectable trademark.[19] Qualitex created dry cleaning pads that were greenish gold in color. The color set Qualitex's dry cleaning pads apart from its competitor's cream color dry cleaning pads. The Supreme Court characterized the use of the greenish gold color as descriptive. Accordingly, to be afforded trademark protection, the Supreme Court queried whether the use of the color had obtained secondary meaning. The Court found that the color mark had obtained secondary meaning because there was evidence that consumers associated the green dry-cleaning pads with Qualitex. Thus, the color mark was protectable under trademark law.

Whether a mark has obtained secondary meaning is a question of fact. The decision maker may rely on direct evidence and circumstantial evidence. Direct evidence typically manifests itself in the form of consumer surveys. Consumer surveys are statistical evidence of whether consumers associate a product or service with a mark.

---

[18] Zatarains, Inc. v. Oak Grove Smokehouse, Inc., 698 F.2d 786, 790 (5th Cir. 1983) abrogated by KP Permanent Make-Up, Inc. v. Lasting Impression I, Inc., 543 U.S. 111, 125 S. Ct. 542, 160 L. Ed. 2d 440 (2004).

[19] *Qualitex Co. v. Jacobson Prods. Co.*, 514 U.S. 159, 161, 115 S. Ct. 1300, 1302 (1995).

Circumstantial evidence may also establish that a trademark has obtained secondary meaning. Circumstantial evidence of secondary meaning may include facts related to how the owner has used her mark in commerce. Such facts may include advertising expenses, how long the mark has been used in association with particular goods and services being sold in commerce, and the geographic regions in which the mark is being used.

Generic Terms

A generic term identifies a general category of goods or services. Generic terms lie opposite inherently distinctive marks on the distinctiveness spectrum. If a term is generic, it is not eligible for trademark protection.

Whether a term is generic depends on the genus of goods or services at issue and whether the relevant public understands that the term refers to that genus of goods or services.[20] For example, a "PENCIL" is the generic name for a writing instrument. The word "ESCALATOR" is the generic name for a machine with moveable stairs for transporting people from one level to another level.

A word or phrase may be generic on its face. It may also become generic over time. The term "genericide" denotes when a mark transitions from protectable to generic. Examples of popular word marks that have become generic include, "ELEVATOR," "REFRIGERATOR," and "TRAMPOLINE." Genericide is a defense to trademark infringement and is discussed in further detail in Chapter 3.

Limitations on Trademark Subject Matter

Federal law prohibits the registration of certain subject matter as trademarks.[21] Specifically, it bars the registration of marks that:

- contain ~~immoral~~, deceptive ~~or scandalous~~ matter ~~or are disparaging~~[22]

- contain the insignia of the United States, states, municipalities, or foreign governments,

- contain the name, portrait, or signature identifying a particular living individual except by his written

---

[20] H. Marvin Ginn Corp. v. Int'l Ass'n of Fire Chiefs, Inc., 782 F.2d 987, 990, 228 USPQ 528, 530 (Fed. Cir. 1986).

[21] 15 U.S.C. § 1052(a).

[22] *See* Matal v. Tam, 137 S. Ct. 1744 (2017) (holding that the disparagement clause is invalid under First Amendment protection of free speech); *see also* In re Brunetti, 877 F.3d 1330, 1355 (C.A.Fed., 2017) (finding that there is no "substantial government interest justifying the § 2(a) bar on immoral or scandalous marks.").

consent, or the name, signature, or portrait of a
deceased President of the United States during the life
of his widow, if any, except by the written consent of
the widow

- are likely to cause confusion with a non-abandoned
  mark

- are descriptive or deceptively misdescriptive

- are primarily geographically descriptive

- are primarily geographically deceptively descriptive

- are primarily merely a surname

- are functional

This chapter discussed descriptive marks in the section on
marks that require secondary meaning. Chapter 3 discusses marks
that are likely to cause confusion in the context of trademark
infringement. This section summarizes the law on other barred
subject matter.

Immoral, Deceptive, Scandalous, and Disparaging Matter

In the last year, significant changes have occurred in this area
of law. As of the publication of this book, courts have held that
barring the registration of immoral, scandalous, and disparaging
matter is unconstitutional. Because of its importance, this section
summarizes the Supreme Court case responsible for these recent
developments.

Before understanding how the law has changed, it's important
to understand what was considered immoral, scandalous, and
disparaging under the statute. The law characterizes immoral or
scandalous matter as shocking, offensive or vulgar. Deceptive subject
matter falsely describes material characteristics of a good or service.
Finally, the disparagement clause barred registration of marks that
disparage "persons, living dead, institutions, beliefs, or national
symbols, or bring them into contempt, or disrepute."[23]

In a recent opinion, the United States Supreme Court held that
the disparagement clause of Section 2(a) is unconstitutional because
it violates First Amendment protection of free speech.[24] The mark at
issue in the case was "THE SLANTS." THE SLANTS is the name of
an Asian-American rock band and also recognized as a racial slur.
The band chose the name to reclaim the slur and make a statement

---

[23] 15 U.S.C. § 1052(a).
[24] Matal v. Tam, 137 S. Ct. 1744 (2017).

about broader issues of race in the United States.[25] In 2011, Simon Shiao Tam, one of the band members, filed an application to register THE SLANTS mark.

The USPTO rejected the registration of THE SLANTS mark on the grounds that it was disparaging to Asian-Americans. This decision seemed to align with others where the USPTO had rejected so-called disparaging marks for registration including "STOP THE ISLAMISATION OF AMERICA," "SQUAW VALLEY," and "N.I.G.G.A. NATURALLY INTELLIGENT GOD GIFTED AFRICANS."

The district court held that Section 2(a) did not violate Tam's first amendment rights because the bar to registration did not prevent Tam from using THE SLANTS in association with his band and music. Sitting *en banc*, the Federal Circuit disagreed and held that because the First Amendment protects "even hurtful speech" the USPTO could not bar registration of disparaging marks under Section 2(a) of the Latham Act.

The Supreme Court affirmed, finding that the disparagement clause violates the Free Speech Clause of the First Amendment. Similarly, in December of 2017, the U.S. Court of Appeals for the Federal Circuit held that the barring marks for being immoral or scandalous was also unconstitutional because it violates the First Amendment.[26]

Deceptively Misdescriptive Marks

The Lanham Act prohibits the registration of marks that are deceptively misdescriptive.[27] A mark is deceptively misdescriptive when (1) it immediately conveys a false idea "of an ingredient, quality, characteristic, function, or feature" about its associated goods or services and (2) people are likely to believe the misrepresentation.[28] Barring deceptively misdescriptive marks aligns with a core goal of trademark law—consumer protection. Consider the following example.

A car manufacturer uses the word TITANIUM in association with its vehicles. Consumers believe that the car manufacturer's vehicles are made of TITANIUM. But, the vehicles at issue are not

---

[25] *Id.* at 1754.

[26] In re Brunetti, 877 F.3d 1330, 1357 (C.A.Fed., 2017).

[27] 15 U.S.C. § 1052(e)(1).

[28] Trademark Man. of Exam. Proc. 1209.04 (8th ed. 2017).

made of nor do they contain titanium. In this case, the car manufacturer's use of TITANIUM is deceptively misdescriptive.[29]

Geographic Marks

Primarily Geographically Descriptive Marks

Section 2(e)(2) of the Lanham Act prohibits the registration of marks that are primarily geographically descriptive. A mark is considered primarily geographically descriptive if (1) the primary significance of the mark is a generally known geographic location, (2) the goods or services originate in the place identified in the mark and (3) it is likely that purchasers believe the goods or services originate in the geographic place identified by the mark.[30] For example, the "Bank of Texas" is primarily geographically descriptive of a bank located in Texas.

An exception to § 2(e)(2) is that marks that indicate regional origin may be registrable as collective or certification marks. Also, if a primarily geographically descriptive mark has obtained secondary meaning, then it is registrable. "PINEHURST" is an example of a geographically descriptive term for a locale in North Carolina that has obtained secondary meaning as a service mark for identifying resort and golf services.[31]

Primarily Geographically Deceptively Misdescriptive Marks

Section 2(e)(3) bars the registration of primarily geographically deceptively misdescriptive marks. A mark is primarily geographically deceptively misdescriptive if (1) the primary significance of the mark is a generally known geographic location, (2) the goods or services do not originate in the place identified in the mark, (3) purchasers would be likely to believe that the goods or services originate in the geographic place identified in the mark, and (4) the misrepresentation is a material factor in a significant portion of the relevant consumer's decision to buy the goods or use the services.[32] For example, the U.S. Court of Appeals for the Federal Circuit upheld a decision refusing the registration of a mark containing the word "PARIS" because the only connection the fashion accessories associated with the mark had to Paris was that they were designed by a French citizen who lived in Paris but currently resided

---

[29] Glendale Int'l Corp. v. United States PTO, 374 F. Supp. 2d 479, 487 (E.D. Va. 2005).

[30] Trademark Man. of Exam. Proc. 1210.01(a) (8th ed. 2017).

[31] Resorts of Pinehurst, Inc. v. Pinehurst Nat'l Corp., 148 F.3d 417, 422 (4th Cir. 1998).

[32] Trademark Man. of Exam. Proc. 1210.01(b) (8th ed. 2017).

in the U.S.[33] The court relied heavily on the fact that consumers would think of Paris as known for fashion accessories and that the applicant's goods were not designed or manufactured in Paris.[34] Thus, this case is another illustration of how trademark law attempts to protect consumers.

Surnames

Individuals may desire to use their name in business, and many people share the same names. Section 2(e)(4) of the Lanham Act bars the registration of marks that are primarily merely a surname absent a showing of secondary meaning. Thus, the law requires that a surname such as "Smith" obtain secondary meaning before registration on the Principal Register.[35]

The Functionality Doctrine

The functionality doctrine states that a useful product feature cannot be a protectable trademark. A product feature is functional if it is essential to the use or purpose of the product or it affects its cost and quality.[36] The doctrine prevents trademark law from protecting a feature that is better suited for patent protection. It also prevents protection of features that are useful as more than just a source identifier.

In limited cases, the functionality doctrine may prevent color from being used as a trademark. The reflective colors used for traffic signs are functional because the color makes the signs visible to drivers and pedestrians.

Note that in *Qualitex*, the trademarked green and gold color for the dry-cleaning pads did not run afoul of the functionality doctrine. There was no evidence that the green color provided any functional difference in the use of the dry-cleaning pad during the dry-cleaning process. The color did not get clothes cleaner nor did it make the process faster. Instead, the color identified Qualitex as the source of the dry-cleaning pads.

---

[33] In re Miracle Tuesday, LLC, 695 F.3d 1339, 1344 (Fed. Cir. 2012).

[34] *Id.* at 1345.

[35] Surnames capable of obtaining secondary meaning may be registered on the Supplemental register. For more information on the Principal and Supplemental Register see Chapter 2.

[36] Traffix Devices v. Marketing Displays, Inc. 532 U.S. 23 (2001).

TRADEMARK SUBJECT MATTER CHECKLIST

With the above Review in mind, the Trademark Subject Matter Checklist is presented below.

A. IDENTIFY THE TYPE OF MARK. Determine how to categorize a mark associated with goods or services.

  1. Trademark. A trademark is any word, name, symbol or device, or any combination thereof used or which a person has a bona fide intention to use in commerce to identify and distinguish her goods or indicate the source of goods.

  2. Service Mark. A service mark is any word, name, symbol, or device or combination thereof that are used to identify and distinguish the services of one person and to indicate the source of the services.

  3. Nontraditional Marks. Nontraditional marks are subject matter eligible for trademark protection such as sounds, smells, texture, motion, and color that are used to identify and distinguish goods or services and to indicate the source of the goods and services.

  4. Certification Mark. A certification mark is any word, name, symbol, or device or combination thereof that is used to certify (1) origin, (2) other characteristics of the good or service such as material, mode of manufacture, quality, accuracy or (3) that the labor on the goods and services was performed by members of a union or other organization.

  5. Collective Mark. A collective mark is a trademark or service mark used by a member of an organization to denote membership or affiliation with that organization or to identify the goods and services of the members of the organization.

  6. Trade Dress and Product Packaging. Trade dress protects the overall appearance of a product (the product design) or a product's packaging.

  7. Trade Name. A trade name is any name used by a person to identify a business or vocation. Unless they are associated with a good or service, trade names cannot be registered as trademarks under federal law. However, trade names can be protected under common law and may be registered under state trademark law.

B. **DETERMINE THE DISTINCTIVENESS OF THE SUBJECT MATTER.** Determine whether the subject matter at issue is inherently distinctive, requires secondary meaning or is generic. This determination must be made by considering the subject matter in relation to the associated goods or services.

1. **Inherently Distinctive.** Marks that are suggestive, arbitrary or fanciful are considered inherently distinctive. Inherently distinctive marks are automatically eligible for trademark protection.

    a. **Fanciful.** A fanciful mark is an invented word or phrase that has no dictionary meaning.

    b. **Arbitrary.** An arbitrary mark makes use of a common word that does not describe the associated good or service.

    c. **Suggestive.** Suggestive marks require imagination to associate the mark with the good or service.

2. **Marks That Require Secondary Meaning.** For some subject matter to be eligible for trademark protection, the law requires proof that the subject matter has become distinctive with respect to its associated goods or services. This is referred to as acquired distinctiveness or secondary meaning.

    a. **Subject Matter.** Descriptive terms, geographically descriptive terms, personal names and nontraditional trademarks such as colors may be registered and protected as trademarks if they have acquired secondary meaning.

    b. **Evidence of Secondary Meaning.** Whether a mark has acquired secondary meaning is a question of fact and can be proven by direct and circumstantial evidence. Consumer surveys are commonly used as direct evidence of secondary meaning. Circumstantial evidence of secondary meaning may include facts related to how the mark was used in commerce, e.g., advertising expenses, the length of use, and geographic scope of use.

3. **Generic Terms.** Generic terms identify a category of goods or services and are not eligible for trademark protection. A word or phrase may be generic on its face or it may become generic over time. Genericide occurs when a mark transitions from protectable to generic.

a. **Genus.** Determine what is the genus of the goods or services at issue.

b. **Public Understanding.** Determine if the relevant public understands the term to primarily refer to that genus of goods or services.

C. **CONSIDER THE RELEVANT LIMITATIONS ON TRADEMARK SUBJECT MATTER.** Certain subject matter is not protectable under trademark law and is generally barred from federal registration if it consists of the following:

1. **Deceptive Matter.** Deceptive subject matter falsely describes material characteristics of a good or service. Note that the Supreme Court recently held that barring immoral, scandalous, and disparaging marks from registration violates the First Amendment and is therefore unconstitutional.

2. **Insignia of the United States, States, Municipalities, or Foreign Governments.** Self-explanatory.

3. **A Name, Portrait, or Signature Identifying a Particular Living Individual Except by His Written Consent.** Self-explanatory.

4. **A Name, Signature, or Portrait of a deceased President of the United States During the Life of His Widow, if Any, Except by the Written Consent of the Widow.** Self-explanatory.

5. **A Mark That is Likely to Cause Confusion with a Non-abandoned Mark.** *See* Chapter 3, *infra.*

6. **A Descriptive Mark.** A descriptive mark describes qualities of an associated good or service which do not identify and distinguish the source of the associated products or services.

   a. **Test for Descriptiveness.** A term is descriptive if it immediately conveys a feature, characteristic, ingredient or function of the associated goods or services.

   b. **Secondary Meaning.** If a mark is descriptive then in order to be eligible for trademark protection, the law requires that the mark have secondary meaning. A mark has obtained secondary meaning when the consuming public associates the mark with a particular product or a specific source of goods.

7. **A Mark Which Is Deceptively Misdescriptive.** A mark is deceptively misdescriptive when (1) it immediately conveys a false idea "of an ingredient, quality, characteristic, function, or feature" about the goods or services and (2) people are likely to believe the misrepresentation.

8. **A Mark Which Is Primarily Geographically Descriptive.** A mark is primarily geographically descriptive if (1) the primary significance of the mark is a generally known geographic location, (2) the goods or services originate in the place identified in the mark and (3) it is likely that purchasers believe the goods or services originate in the geographic place identified by the mark. Primarily Geographically Descriptive marks may be registrable if they have obtained secondary meaning or indicate regional origin as collective or certification marks.

9. **A Mark Which Is Primarily Geographically Deceptively Descriptive.** A mark is primarily geographically deceptively misdescriptive if (1) the primary significance of the mark is a generally known geographic location, (2) the goods or services do not originate in the place identified in the mark, (3) purchasers would be likely to believe that the goods or services originate in the geographic place identified in the mark, and (4) the misrepresentation is a material factor in a significant portion of the relevant consumer's decision to buy the goods or use the services.

10. **A Mark Which Is Merely a Surname.** The law bars registration of surnames unless they have acquired secondary meaning in association with specific goods or services.

11. **Comprises Matter That Is Functional.** Subject matter that comprises a useful product feature cannot be registered as a trademark. A product feature is functional if it is essential to the use or purpose of the product or it affects its cost and quality.

ILLUSTRATIVE PROBLEMS

Here are two problems that illustrate how the Checklist can be used to resolve trademark subject matter questions.

■ PROBLEM 1.1 ■

Christian Louboutin, a women's footwear designer, produces and sells women's high heel shoes. Louboutin paints the outsole of the shoes with a high-gloss red lacquer. The red contrasts with the color of the rest of the shoe. For almost thirty years, Louboutin's company has invested time and money to promote his designer high heels. As a result, consumers associate the red outsole on women's high heels with Louboutin.

Is the red lacquer outsole a protectable trademark? Why or why not?

Analysis

To answer PROBLEM 1.1, you must determine whether the subject matter at issue is protectable as a trademark. For subject matter to be protectable as a trademark, it must be either (1) inherently distinctive or (2) have obtained secondary meaning. Inherently distinctive marks intrinsically serve as an identifier of goods or services and are automatically eligible for trademark protection. Alternatively, a mark has obtained secondary meaning when the consuming public associates the subject mark with a particular product or a specific source of goods.

The mark at issue here is the red color of a shoe's outsole. The red color contrasts with the color of the rest of the shoe. As stated in *Qualitex*, trademark law does not preclude the use of color as a trademark. However, for a color to be protectable, it must have obtained secondary meaning.

Several factors can be used as evidence of secondary meaning including (1) advertising expenditures, (2) consumer studies, (3) unsolicited media attention, (4) sales success, (5) attempts by others to copy the mark, and (6) length and exclusivity of the mark's use. Here, there is evidence that Louboutin made significant investments in advertising, experienced successful sales, and that the contrasting red outsole became closely associated with his name and fashion house. Thus, the evidence supports a conclusion that the contrasting red outsole has obtained secondary meaning and is, therefore, protectable as a trademark.[37]

■ **PROBLEM 1.2** ■

Sal's Pizzeria is a twenty-five-year-old pizza restaurant founded by Sal. Mario has worked for Sal's Pizzeria for the last ten years as a cook. Sal fired Mario in 2016. Shortly after his firing, Mario opened his owned pizza restaurant called Mario's. Sal acquired evidence that Mario is using Sal's recipes and cooking manuals to make pizza that is being sold at Mario's. Sal's Pizzeria sues Mario's, asserting that the flavor of Sal's Pizzeria pizza is a protected trademark.

---

[37] *See* Christian Louboutin S.A. v. Yves Saint Laurent Am. Holdings, Inc., 696 F.3d 206 (2d Cir. 2012).

Can the flavor of pizza be a protectable trademark? Why or why not?

Analysis

Like PROBLEM 1.1, here you must determine whether the subject matter at issue, the flavor of pizza, is protectable as a trademark. Anything that has meaning can be protectable as a trademark. There is not an explicit prohibition on flavor being used as a trademark. However, the subject matter at issue must also distinguish the source of goods and should not run afoul of any limitations mentioned earlier in this chapter.

In order for subject matter to be protectable as a trademark it must be either (1) inherently distinctive or (2) have obtained secondary meaning. Inherently distinctive marks intrinsically serve as an identifier of goods or services and are automatically eligible for trademark protection. Alternatively, a mark has obtained secondary meaning when the consuming public associates the subject mark with a particular product or a specific source of goods.

Flavor and color are similar in that they are both considered characteristics of goods. Color may be used as a trademark if it has obtained secondary meaning. Similarly, flavor cannot serve as a trademark unless it has obtained secondary meaning. Thus, Sal's Pizzeria would need to present evidence that the consuming public associated the flavor of its pizza with Sal's Pizzeria as the source. Unfortunately for Sal, even if that evidence exists, he has another problem that will prohibit him from using flavor as a trademark.

Flavor as it is associated with food, may be functional. The functionality doctrine states that a useful product feature cannot be protected by trademark law. A product feature is functional if it is essential to the use or purpose of the product or it affects its cost and quality. For example, flavoring medicine to make it taste better and easier to consume is a functional use of flavoring that would make the taste ineligible for trademark protection.[38]

With food such as pizza, customers mostly consume it for the flavor. Flavor affects the cost and quality of food. Better tasting food is perceived to be of higher quality and can command premium pricing. The flavor of Sal's Pizzeria pizza is a functional element and thus, unprotectable as a trademark.[39]

---

[38] In re N.V. Organon, 79 U.S.P.Q.2d 1639 at *6–13.

[39] *See* N.Y. Pizzeria, Inc. v. Syal, 56 F. Supp. 3d 875 (S.D. Tex. 2014)

POINTS TO REMEMBER

- A trademark is generally, any word, name, symbol, or device that is used to identify or distinguish the source of goods.

- Generic marks are ineligible for trademark protection. Descriptive marks require secondary meaning to be protectable as trademarks. Inherently distinctive marks are automatically eligible for protection.

- Trade dress protects the overall appearance of a product (the product design) or a product's packaging. A person seeking to protect a product design under trade dress must show that the design has obtained secondary meaning. In contrast, product packaging may be inherently distinctive.

- The Supreme Court recently held that a mark cannot be barred from registration for being disparaging under section 2 of the Lanham Act. Similarly, a federal appeals court has recently held that barring the registration of immoral or scandalous marks is also unconstitutional.

- Functional subject matter is not eligible for trademark protection.

CHAPTER 2

Obtaining Trademark Rights

After covering trademark subject matter, a typical IP course will examine the process for obtaining legal rights in a trademark. Obtaining trademark rights can involve both common law and federal law. Understanding how to secure legally enforceable rights in a trademark and the relationship between the common law and federal registration requirements is vital to a student's success on IP exams. This chapter summarizes the law for obtaining trademark rights in a way that will allow you to systematically identify the issues and apply the correct legal rules to most exam questions. This chapter also briefly summarizes the law governing how a trademark owner can maintain rights in her mark and under what circumstances she may lose rights in her trademark.

OBTAINING TRADEMARK RIGHTS REVIEW

Obtaining Trademark Rights

The owner of a mark may obtain legally protectable trademark rights under common law and federally register their trademark to obtain additional benefits that come with federal registration. This section summarizes the requirements for obtaining common law rights in a mark. It then details how the federal registration system for trademarks works. Finally, this section summarizes the federal trademark procedures typically explored in an IP survey course.

Use

"The right to a trademark comes from its use."[1] To establish protectable rights in a trademark, the owner of the mark must (1) use the mark in commerce or (2) federally register the mark and demonstrate his bona fide intent to use the mark in commerce. The latter procedure requires a hopeful mark owner to file an "intent-to-use" application with the USPTO. The application procedures will be

---

[1] 1–3 Gilson on Trademarks § 3.02[2][a] (2017).

summarized later in this chapter. In sum, use in commerce is the key to establishing protectable trademark rights and acquiring a federally registered mark.[2]

A mark must be used in connection with a good or service to be protectable.[3] To "use" a mark means that the goods or services associated with the mark are sold to the public with the mark attached or referenced. A public sale serves a notice function. It puts other producers on notice that the mark in use is associated with goods or services. In addition, public sales serve to link the mark with the associated goods or services in the minds of consumers. In limited circumstances, the use of a mark in advertising or promotion, without sales, may also be enough to establish a use in commerce of the mark.

Sufficient use of a mark in commerce may establish the owner's common law rights in the mark. To determine whether use of a mark is sufficient to establish common law rights, courts have examined a number of factors including: (1) whether the use was a bonafide use or a token use performed in an attempt to establish rights, (2) the type and volume of sales, (3) the public nature of the sales, and (4) whether the sales were continuous.[4]

Common law rights in a trademark are limited to the market where the goods and services associated with the mark are sold. The scope of the market is defined by sales, the reputation or business presence, and the possible zone of expansion. Statutory protections for unregistered common law trademarks is set forth in Section 43(a) of the Lanham Act. These common law rights are separate and distinct from federal registration.[5]

Use of a mark in *interstate* commerce permits a mark owner to apply for a federally registered trademark. Successful federal registration gives the mark owner nationwide rights in his mark. The federal registration process is described later in this chapter. The following section summarizes the concept of "priority" as it relates to trademark use.

Priority

The date upon which a mark was first used in commerce is the mark's priority date. In a dispute between two parties that assert rights in the same mark or confusingly similar marks, the party that

---

[2] 1–3 Gilson on Trademarks § 3.02[1] (2017).

[3] *See* United Drug Co. v. Rectanus Co. 248 U.S. 90, 97, 39 S. Ct. 48, 50 (1918)("There is no such thing as property in a trade-mark except as a right appurtenant to an established business or trade in connection with which the mark is employed.").

[4] 1–3 Gilson on Trademarks § 3.02[2][a][ii] (2017).

[5] 1–3 Gilson on Trademarks § 3.02[2][a] (2017).

was the first to use the mark in commerce has superior (possibly exclusive) rights in the mark. This senior user can enforce his rights in the trademark against subsequent users.

A small amount of use may be sufficient to establish a priority date if it is followed by continuous commercial use. The amount of products sold and whether those sales are followed by an application for registration also have an impact on whether an owner has exclusive rights to a mark. For example, in *ZAZU Designs v. L'Oreal, S.A.,* the court held that a small amount of sales followed by an application to register a mark was insufficient to establish exclusive nationwide rights in the mark as of the day of the first sale.[6] A substantial amount of sales may also be enough to establish exclusive nationwide rights in the mark.

Federal Trademark Registration

An owner of a valid trademark can register the mark with the USPTO. This section will first describe the two federal trademark databases. Next, this section summarizes the two types of applications for federal registration—Use-Based Applications and Intent to Use Applications. Finally, this section will cover grounds for refusing the registration of a trademark.

The Supplemental and Principal Registers

An applicant's trademark may be recorded on one of two federal registers—the Principal Register or the Supplemental Register. Marks placed on the Supplemental Register are words, shapes, symbols, trade dress, etc., that are capable of distinguishing an applicant's goods or services but cannot be registered on the Principal Register primarily because they lack distinctiveness.[7] Another function of the supplemental register is to enable U.S. applicants to register marks in other countries.[8]

In contrast, the Principal Register records valid trademarks, service marks, certification marks, and collective marks that are distinctive. An owner of a trademark recorded on the Principal Register acquires several legal benefits. Registration on the Principal Register is prima facie evidence of the validity of the mark and ownership. Registration on the Principal Register also serves as nationwide constructive notice of ownership and use of the mark. A

---

[6] ZAZU Designs v. L'Oreal, S.A., 979 F.2d 499, 503 (7th Cir. 1992)("A few bottles sold over the counter in Hinsdale, and a few more mailed to friends in Texas and Florida, neither link the ZAZU mark with ZHD's product in the minds of consumers nor put other producers on notice.").

[7] 15 U.S.C. § 1091(a).

[8] 1–4 Gilson on Trademarks § 4.07[01][2][0a] (2017).

mark on the Principal Register is also eligible to obtain "incontestability" status.[9] The owner of a mark on the Principal Register has the right to bring a federal cause of action without regard to diversity or minimum amounts in controversy and may also obtain enhanced remedies in federal court. Finally, the owner of a mark registered on the Principal Register has the ability to request that the government stop the importation of articles bearing an infringing mark.

Use-Based Applications

If an applicant has used a mark in interstate commerce, they may file a use-based application to register their trademark with the USPTO. The application includes information about the mark such as the date of first use, a description of the goods and services associated with the mark, a drawing of the mark, and a specimen. A specimen shows the way in which the mark will be seen by the public.[10] Once received by the Office, a trademark attorney reviews the trademark application to determine whether the subject mark is eligible for registration. Among other criteria, the examining attorney will evaluate whether the subject mark is barred from registration under Section 2 of the Lanham Act (15 U.S.C. § 1052).

After the application has been examined and satisfied the trademark attorney's requirements, if the application is for registration on the Principal Register, the USPTO publishes information about the application in the Official Gazette. During a thirty-day period after publication of the mark, third parties have an opportunity file a Notice of Opposition to the mark.[11] Assuming a third party does not file a Notice of Opposition to the mark within the thirty-day period, the USPTO will issue a Certificate of Registration for the applicant's trademark.

Intent-to-Use Applications

An applicant may use an Intent-to-Use application to register a trademark before it is used in commerce, if the applicant has a bona fide intent to use the mark in commerce. In order to demonstrate an applicant's bona fide intent, the applicant may present evidence such as a business plan, sample products or images from his future website with the product and associated mark. This provision allows parties to file an application for registration before selling a product or service to the public associated with the mark.

---

[9] Incontestability will be discussed later in this chapter.

[10] 8–900 Gilson on Trademarks 904 (2017).

[11] For more information on the Notice of Opposition see the section on Inter Partes Proceedings *infra*.

Examination of an Intent-to-Use application is a two-stage process. In the first stage, the USPTO determines whether the mark is eligible for registration. The second stage requires the applicant to demonstrate that the mark was subsequently used in commerce by filing a Statement of Use. After review of the Statement of Use, the examining attorney may issue a Certificate of Registration for the trademark.[12]

Grounds for Refusing Registration

During the examination of a trademark application, the examining attorney may refuse to register the subject mark on several grounds. Specifically, Section 2 of the Lanham Act bars the registration of marks that (1) contain ~~immoral,~~ deceptive ~~or scandalous~~ matter ~~or are disparaging~~,[13] (2) contain the insignia of the United States, states, municipalities, or foreign governments, (3) contain the name, portrait, or signature identifying a particular living individual except by his written consent, or the name, signature, or portrait of a deceased President of the United States during the life of his widow, if any, except by the written consent of the widow, (4) are likely to cause confusion with a non-abandoned mark, (5) are descriptive or deceptively misdescriptive, (6) are primarily geographically descriptive, are primarily geographically deceptively descriptive, (7) are primarily merely a surname, or (8) are functional.[14]

Bars to registration for deceptive marks, descriptive marks, and functional marks are discussed *supra* in Chapter 1. Marks that are likely to cause confusion will be discussed *infra* in Chapter 3. The remaining bars to registration are self-explanatory.

Maintaining Trademark Rights

This section summarizes the most common post-registration trademark procedures covered in an IP survey course. After a trademark has obtained a certificate of registration on the Principal Register, there are procedures the owner must perform to maintain his trademark. After registration, there are also procedures an owner can take to strengthen his mark. Finally, this section describes ways in which third parties can challenge the validity of another's trademark through inter pares proceedings.

---

[12] Under an Intent-to-Use process, the trademark's priority date is the date upon which the Intent-to-Use application was filed.

[13] *See* Chapter 1, *supra*, for a discussion of why immoral, scandalous, and disparaging marks are now eligible for registration.

[14] 15 U.S.C. § 1052.

Maintenance Filings

An owner of a federally registered trademark is required to make maintenance filings at specified intervals. This section summarizes the Section 8 Declaration of Use and the Section 9 Renewal of Registration maintenance filings.

Section 8 Declaration of Use

A Section 8 Declaration of Use is a sworn statement by the owner indicating that she continues to use the registered trademark or that the trademark is not in use in commerce due to special circumstances that excuse nonuse. In addition to the sworn statement, the owner is required to submit a specimen, a filing fee, and notify the USPTO of any goods and services no longer being associated with the mark. The Section 8 Declaration must be filed between the fifth and sixth years after a certificate of registration has been issued, between the ninth and tenth years after a certificate of registration has been issued and then every ten years thereafter.

Section 9 Renewal of Registration

A Section 9 Renewal of Registration is a written request by the owner to keep her trademark registration active. The owner must file a Section 9 Declaration between the ninth and tenth years after a certificate of registration has been issued and then every ten years after.

Incontestability

After a trademark has been federally registered for five years, it is eligible for incontestability status. A trademark's incontestable status provides conclusive evidence of a trademark owner's exclusive right to use the trademark. Because it provides certain legal advantages, the ability to obtain an incontestable trademark rewards diligent trademark owners. In order to be eligible for incontestability status, a trademark must also be registered on the Principal Register and must not have been the subject of any adverse decisions or proceedings.

A trademark owner obtains several legal advantages when her trademark becomes incontestable. During litigation, an incontestable mark provides for more predictability and narrows the legal issues that may arise. Once a trademark obtains incontestability status, third party attacks on the trademark's validity are limited in scope.[15] For example, in *Park 'N Fly, Inc. V. Dollar Park & Fly, Inc.*, the Supreme Court found that the trademark

---

[15] 1–4 Gilson on Trademarks § 4.03 (2017).

"Park 'N Fly" was incontestable and therefore the defendant could not assert that Park 'N Fly was descriptive as a defense to trademark infringement.[16]

However, an incontestable trademark is not invincible. It is still vulnerable to challenges on the grounds that the trademark was obtained by fraud, the trademark has been abandoned, the trademark is generic, the trademark is functional or that the trademark has been used to misrepresent the source of goods or services.

Inter Partes Proceedings

IP survey students should be aware of four inter partes trademark procedures—interferences, concurrent use proceedings, cancellations, and oppositions. This section summarizes those procedures.

Notice of Opposition

Before a mark is federally registered, a third party may challenge its registration using the Notice of Opposition procedure. A third party may file a Notice of Opposition to a trademark registration up to thirty days after the USPTO publishes the mark in the Official Gazette. A third party filing a Notice of Opposition must demonstrate that they are likely to be damaged by registration of the mark in question and there are valid legal grounds why the applicant is not entitled to register the mark. These valid legal grounds may include any bar to registration under Section 2, dilution, or that the applicant's mark has not been sufficiently used in interstate commerce. Generally, oppositions are handled by the Trademark Trial and Appeal Board (TTAB). An opposition may result in the granting of the trademark application, amendments being made to the application, or the application being rejected.

Cancellation

Unlike oppositions, a cancellation proceeding applies to trademarks that have already received a certificate of registration. A third party may petition the USPTO to cancel a trademark if he believes that he will be damaged by the mark's federal registration.[17] When a trademark is cancelled, all rights in the mark are extinguished. Up to five years after registration, the USPTO may cancel a trademark under any valid legal grounds. Five years after

---

[16] Park 'N Fly, Inc. v. Dollar Park & Fly, Inc., 469 U.S. 189, 196, 105 S. Ct. 658, 662, 83 L. Ed. 2d 582 (1985) ("The language of the Lanham Act also refutes any conclusion that an incontestable mark may be challenged as merely descriptive.").

[17] A court may also cancel a trademark in a civil lawsuit.

registration, a trademark may only be canceled for fraud, abandonment, functionality, or genericide.

Interferences

Interferences Proceedings concern conflicting applications or an application that conflicts with a registered but yet incontestable trademark. The purpose of the Interference Proceeding is to determine which trademark is entitled to registration. A third party may initiate an Interference Proceeding up to five years after a mark is published in the Official Gazette.

Concurrent Registration

If an applicant is aware of an existing trademark or an applied for trademark similar to the applicant's mark, she may file a petition for concurrent registration. In the concurrent registration process, the USPTO balances the first use of a mark with first registration to determine whether two similar marks should be concurrently registered. If the USPTO determines to register two marks concurrently, they may be subjected to use limitations. For example, the USPTO may impose geographic restrictions on where each mark can be used to avoid confusion.

Loss of Trademark Rights

There are several ways that a trademark owner may lose his rights in his trademark. The most common ways are: cancelation, abandonment, genericide, and naked licensing. Cancelation was discussed *supra* in the section on inter partes proceedings. Remember that in addition to the USPTO procedure, a trademark may be canceled as the result of a lawsuit. An owner may also lose rights in his trademark by abandonment, genericide, or naked licensing. Abandonment, genercide, and naked licensing are common defenses to trademark infringement and are summarized in Chapter 3.

 OBTAINING TRADEMARK RIGHTS CHECKLIST

With the above Review in mind, the Obtaining Trademark Rights Checklist is presented below.

A. DETERMINE WHAT RIGHTS HAVE BEEN ESTABLISHED IN THE TRADEMARK. Determine if the owner of the trademark has established common law and federal rights in the trademark.

1. **Use.** Has the trademark been used in commerce in association with a good or service? A trademark's use in commerce establishes protectable common law trademark rights and is important for federal registration. The common law rights are limited to the market where the mark is used. Use of a mark in interstate commerce can be the first step in obtaining federally registered trademark rights.

2. **Priority.** Who used the mark in commerce first? The party that was the first to use a mark in commerce is the senior user and has superior rights in the mark. The date a mark is first used is its priority date. Was the use substantial enough to establish rights in the mark? A small amount of use may be sufficient if it is followed by continuous commercial use.

3. **Federal Trademark Registration.** The federal registration of a trademark records a valid trademark. An applicant may file a used-based or intent-to-use application. A trademark attorney will examine a trademark application to determine whether it meets the statutory requirements to be registered. A trademark can be registered on the Principal or Supplemental Register.

   a. **Principal Register.** Distinctive trademarks are registered on the Principal Register. A trademark on the Principal Register acquires several legal benefits. For example, registration on the Principal Register is prima facie evidence of the validity of the mark.

   b. **Supplemental Register.** Trademarks that lack distinctiveness may be registered on the Supplemental Register.

   c. **Use-Based Applications.** If an applicant has used a mark in interstate commerce, they may file a used-based application. After the application has been examined, if the application is for registration on the Principal Register the USPTO publishes information about the application in the Official Gazette. If a third party does not file a Notice of Opposition to the mark within the thirty-day period, the USPTO will issue a Certificate of Registration for the trademark.

   d. **Intent-to-Use Applications.** An applicant may file an intent-to-use application to register a trademark before it is used in commerce if the applicant has a bona fide intent to use the mark in commerce. During the first stage of examination, the trademark attorney determines whether the mark is entitled to registration. After the opposition period, the USPTO issues a Notice of Allowance indicating that the mark has been allowed but is not yet registered. The applicant then has a period of time, extendible up to three years, to use the mark in commerce and file a Statement of Use (SOU) with the USPTO. During the second stage of examination, the trademark examining attorney reviews the applicant's SOU and if the requirements are satisfied, issues a Certificate of Registration.

e. **Grounds for Refusing Registration.** Section 2 of the Lanham Act bars the registration of marks that (1) contain deceptive matter, (2) contain the insignia of the United States, states, municipalities, or foreign governments, (3) contain the name, portrait, or signature identifying a particular living individual except by his written consent, or the name, signature, or portrait of a deceased President of the United States during the life of his widow, if any, except by the written consent of the widow, (4) are likely to cause confusion with a non-abandoned mark, (5) are descriptive or deceptively misdescriptive, (6) are primarily geographically descriptive, are primarily geographically deceptively descriptive, (7) are primarily merely a surname, or (8) are functional. See Chapters 1 and 3 for details on each of the grounds mentioned above.

B. **CONSIDER POST-REGISTRATION TRADEMARK PROCEDURES.** Consider whether the owner of a federally registered trademark has maintained her rights in the trademark. Also, remember that a third party may challenge the owner's rights to the trademark through inter partes proceedings.

1. **Maintenance Filings.** Has the trademark owner made the required maintenance filings at the appropriate times? A Section 8 Declaration of Use indicates that the owner continues to use the registered trademark or that the trademark is not in use due to special circumstances that excuse nonuse. A Section 9 Renewal of Registration is a written request by the applicant to keep her trademark registration active.

2. **Incontestability.** Has the trademark been registered on the Principal Register for five years? If so, it is eligible for incontestability status. Attacks on an incontestable trademark's validity are limited in the scope. However, an incontestable trademark is still vulnerable to challenges on the grounds that the mark was obtained by fraud, the mark has been abandoned, the mark is generic, the mark is functional or that the mark has been used to misrepresent the source of goods or services.

3. **Inter Partes Proceedings.** Inter partes proceedings are internal procedures initiated by interested third parties concerning a trademark application or a registered trademark.

   a. **Opposition.** A third party may file a Notice of Opposition to a trademark registration within thirty days of the mark's publication in the Official Gazette. The third party must demonstrate that they are likely to be damaged by registration of the mark and there are valid legal grounds why the mark should not be registered.

   b. **Cancellation.** A third party may petition the USPTO to cancel a trademark if they believe that they will be damaged by the mark's federal registration. When a trademark is canceled, all rights in the mark are extinguished. The USPTO may cancel a trademark under any valid legal grounds up to five years after it is registered. After five years, a trademark may only be canceled for fraud, abandonment, functionality or genericide.

   c. **Interference.** Interference proceedings concern conflicting trademark applications or a trademark application that conflicts with a registered but yet incontestable mark. The purpose of the interference proceeding is to determine which trademark is entitled to registration. A mark may be subject to an interference proceeding for up to five years after a mark is published in the Official Gazette.

   d. **Concurrent Registration.** If a trademark applicant is aware of an existing trademark or an applied for trademark similar to the applicant's mark, she may file a petition for concurrent registration. If the USPTO determines to register the trademarks concurrently, they are generally subjected to use limitations to avoid consumer confusion.

C. **CONSIDER POTENTIAL LOSS OF RIGHTS IN THE MARK.** Determine whether the trademark owner is vulnerable to losing rights in their mark.

    1. **Cancellation.** When a trademark is canceled, all rights in the mark are extinguished. The USPTO may cancel a trademark under any valid legal grounds up to five years after it is registered. After five years, a trademark may only be canceled for fraud, abandonment, functionality or genericide. A court may also cancel a trademark in a civil lawsuit.

    2. **Abandonment.** Has the trademark owner used the mark in commerce? An owner abandons his trademark if he discontinues using the trademark with no intention to resume use. Nonuse of a trademark for two consecutive years is prima facie evidence of abandonment.

    3. **Genericide.** How is the trademark used by the public? A trademark may become generic over time. Genericide occurs when a mark transitions from protectable to generic. Generic terms are not eligible for trademark protection.

ILLUSTRATIVE PROBLEMS

Here are two problems that illustrate how the Checklist can be used to resolve obtaining trademark rights questions.

■ PROBLEM 2.1 ■

App Amazing is one of the best-selling brands of apple juice in the Unites States. Since 2002, more than 500 million bottles of App Amazing have been sold. App Amazing markets its products in the U.S. and foreign countries under a family of trademarks that include the term "APP." App Amazing's trademark, "APP," was registered on the Principal Register by the USPTO on September 22, 2002, for use with fruit juices.

App Amazing contends it designed its mark to be distinctive and act as a source-identifier. It has invested millions of dollars in the marketing and sale of products under the APP brand. App Amazing asserts that the public associates the APP brand with quality fruit products. The mark "APP" became incontestable in 2007.

Hubert Goddard, d/b/a Appl Beverages ("APPL"), sells a line of apple-flavored energy drinks and snacks. APPL began selling its apple-flavored products labeled "app" in April 2013. App Amazing learned of APPL's activities and informed Goddard of App Amazing's ownership interest in the "APP" brand trademarks. App Amazing requested that APPL change its packaging, explaining that Goddard's use of the word "app" creates a likelihood of confusion among consumers regarding APPL's affiliation, connection, and/or association with App Amazing.

In his defense, Goddard plans to argue that the word mark "APP" is merely descriptive or in the alternative has become generic and is thus unprotectable.

Discuss Goddard's arguments and his likelihood of success.

Analysis

In a trademark infringement suit, the plaintiff must prove that it has a protectable interest in the mark and that the defendant's use of the mark is likely to cause consumer confusion. To answer this question correctly, you do not need to address likelihood of confusion. We will address that issue in chapter 3. You should, however, analyze App Amazing's interest in the "APP" mark and then consider Goddard's arguments.

The facts state that the APP mark was registered in 2002 and became incontestable in 2007. Registration of a mark on the Principal Register is advantageous for several reasons. Registration is prima facie evidence of the validity of the registered mark, the registrant's ownership in the mark and that the owner has the exclusive right to use the mark in commerce in connection with the goods specified in the application. In addition, because a mark is registered, it is presumed that the mark has acquired secondary meaning and is not generic.

Marks may become incontestable five years after they are registered. An incontestable trademark is conclusively presumed valid and to have acquired secondary meaning. Thus, marks that have obtained incontestable status cannot be challenged on the basis that they are merely descriptive. However, incontestable marks are still vulnerable to challenges on the grounds that the mark was obtained by fraud, the mark has been abandoned, the mark is generic, the mark is functional or that the mark has been used to misrepresent the source of goods or services.

Here, App Amazing registered the term "APP" in connection with fruit juices in 2002. Thus, "APP" is presumed valid and App Amazing is presumed to have the exclusive right to use "APP" in connection with fruit juices. Also, because "APP" is registered, it carries the presumption that it is not generic and has acquired secondary meaning. Further, the mark "APP" became incontestable in 2007. Thus, the APP mark cannot be challenged on the basis that it is merely descriptive.

Goddard hopes to argue that the term "APP" is generic or merely descriptive. Unfortunately for Goddard, he will not be able to argue that APP is merely descriptive. The mark "APP" is incontestable and therefore cannot be challenged by a defendant on the grounds that it is merely descriptive. However, Goddard still may be able to assert that the "APP" mark is generic as a defense. In addition, he should consider other grounds for challenging incontestable marks that may be relevant including that the mark was obtained by fraud or that the mark has been used to misrepresent the source of goods or services.

■ PROBLEM 2.2 ■

Sports, Inc. ("SI") sells a wide variety of consumer goods, some of which bear the STICKY trademark. SI claims it was the first to use the STICKY mark as a trademark on sporting goods and athletic shoes.

SI has two federally registered trademarks. Registration No. 2,443,489, issued April 23, 2005, covers "tennis rackets, golf clubs, tennis balls, and golf balls." January 15, 2001 is listed as the date of the mark's "first use" in commerce. Registration No. 2,545,753, issued March 31, 2007, encompasses "bicycles, skateboards, and scooters" and lists January 1, 2002 as the date of first use. However, none of the STICKY registrations mentions athletic shoes or boots.

In 2009, SI began selling an athletic shoe with the STICKY mark affixed to the shoe. On March 28, 2009, SI filed an application to register the mark STICKY for use on "sport and athletic shoes." SI listed January 1, 2005 as the date that STICKY was first used on shoes in commerce. SI claims it has been using the STICKY mark on athletic shoes since at least 2005. In support of this assertion, SI has a 2005 invoice for the sale of athletic shoes that does not indicate the mark the shoes bore and a 2005 internal email that discusses strategy for expanding the STICKY brand to other products, but does not explicitly mention shoes.

Trek Footwear ("Trek") is a California-based company that was founded in 1985. The company manufactures rock climbing shoes. These shoes have soles made of a sticky, high-friction black rubber bearing the trademark STICKY. The STICKY shoes appear exclusively in stores that specialize in outdoor and adventure sports equipment.

Trek began selling STICKY shoes in August 2007 as evidenced by two invoices dated September 5 and 6, to Mekan Shoes in Kearns, Utah and to Climbers Depot in Seattle, Washington. Trek then started advertising STICKY shoes in the March 2008 issue of Outdoor Magazine.

SI sues Trek claiming that Trek's STICKY shoes infringe its rights in the STICKY mark on athletic shoes. In response, Trek moves for summary judgement, arguing that SI is not the senior user of the STICKY mark on athletic shoes.

Discuss which company has priority in the STICKY mark and explain why.

Analysis

First, students should remember that federal registration only records a valid trademark. Trademark rights are acquired by use of the subject mark with the associated goods. The law confers trademark rights to the entity that is the first to use the mark in a commercial transaction.

The use must be associated with a product sold to the public and must be a bona fide, continuous use. The amount of activity depends on the facts, but it must be "sufficiently public to identify or distinguish the marked goods in an appropriate segment of the public mind as those of the adopter of the mark."[18]

SI is not able to rely on its federally registered marks since neither of them mention athletic shoes. Accordingly, SI's argument is that SI began using the STICKY mark in 2005, before Trek, and is therefore the senior user of the mark. In contrast, Trek's argument is that SI is not the senior user of the STICKY mark and therefore Trek does not infringe SI's rights. For the following reasons, Trek is likely to prevail.

Based on the facts, SI cannot show that it was the senior user of the STICKY mark for athletic shoes. To be the senior user of STICKY, SI must show it used STICKY in association with athletic shoes before Trek did in 2007. SI's evidence is insufficient. The 2006 invoices are insufficient evidence of use because they contain no indication that the shoes sold bore the STICKY mark. The email is also no help to SI because it does not mention athletic shoes as a possible target of product expansion. Even if the email did mention athletic shoes, it by itself fails to equal the activity sufficient to conclude that SI used STICKY in association with athletic shoes in commerce.

---

[18] Blue Bell, Inc. v. Farah Mfg. Co., 508 F.2d 1260, 1266 (5th Cir. 1975).

In contrast, there is evidence that Trek began using the mark STICKY in association with athletic shoes in 2007—before SI's sale in 2009. Trek's interstate sales in combination with its advertising activity establish that Trek began using the STICKY mark well before SI's STICKY sales and trademark application was filed. Thus, SI is not the senior user of the mark.

POINTS TO REMEMBER

- Trademark rights in a mark are acquired by use of the mark, not by registration. Common law confers ownership of a trademark to the first person to use the trademark in commerce.

- Federal registration of a trademark is prima facie evidence that the registrant is the owner of the trademark. The registrant is granted a presumption of ownership on the filing date of the federal registration application. Evidence of use of the trademark earlier than the filing date provides the owner with an earlier priority date.

- When a trademark is registered, the registration carries with it a presumption that the trademark has acquired secondary meaning and is not generic.

- A trademark may become incontestable five years after its registration. An incontestable trademark is conclusively presumed valid and cannot be challenged on the grounds that it is merely descriptive.

- Incontestable trademarks are not immune to all legal challenges. Incontestable marks are still vulnerable to challenges on the grounds that the mark was obtained by fraud, the mark has been abandoned, the mark is generic, the mark is functional or that the mark has been used to misrepresent the source of goods or services.

CHAPTER 3

Trademark Infringement

This chapter summarizes the law concerning trademark infringement. The basic question when determining whether a trademark is infringed is whether use of the alleged infringing mark is likely to cause confusion among consumers. This test is rooted in the underlying purpose of trademark law which is to protect and benefit the consuming public. Students should also understand common defenses to infringement such as fair use, functionality, and genericness. This chapter will also summarize dilution, false advertising, cybersquatting and counterfeiting.

TRADEMARK INFRINGEMENT REVIEW

A cause of action for trademark infringement can arise under federal statutes, state statutes, and the common law. The Lanham Act provides for two causes of action for trademark infringement. Section 32 concerns registered marks[1] while § 43 is directed towards unregistered marks.[2]

A party is liable for trademark infringement under § 32(1)(a) if they use a reproduction, counterfeit, copy, or colorable imitation of a registered mark in commerce in connection with the sale, offering for sale, distribution, or advertising of any goods or services that is likely to cause confusion, mistake or deception. Similarly, under § 43(a)(1) of the Lanham Act, a party is liable for trademark infringement if they use "in commerce any word, term, name symbol, or device, or any combination thereof, or any false designation of origin, false or misleading description of fact, or false or misleading representation of fact which is likely to cause confusion, or to cause mistake or to deceive as to affiliation, connection, or association of such person with another person, or as to the origin, sponsorship, or approval or his or her goods, services, or commercial activities by another person."[3]

---

[1] 15 U.S.C. § 1114 (2017).

[2] 15 U.S.C. § 1125 (2017).

[3] Id.

Generally, a cause of action for trademark infringement consist of four elements. First, the claimant must own or have rights in a valid trademark. Second, the defendant must have used the alleged infringing mark. Third, the defendant's use must have been in commerce, in connection with the sale, offering for sale, distribution or advertising of goods or services. Finally, that use must be likely to cause confusion as to the source of goods and services associated with the infringing mark.

Ownership of a Valid Trademark

In order to be successful in a cause of action for trademark infringement, the plaintiff must have a valid trademark. A mark may not be considered a valid trademark for a number of reasons including that it is not protectable subject matter, it has not acquired distinctiveness, or it is barred from registration. Review the previous chapters for summaries of the law regarding these issues. Chapter 1 reviewed subject matter capable of being protected as a trademark. Chapter 2 reviewed the processes for obtaining enforceable rights in trademark subject matter.

Finally, remember that federal registration by itself does not create rights in a mark. Trademark rights are acquired by use. Federal registration on the Principal Register records a valid trademark. Federal registration is prima facie evidence of the marks validity, the registrant's ownership, and the registrant's exclusive right in the mark.

Use in Commerce

Generally, "use" of a trademark means that the trademark was associated with a product or service sold or advertised to the public. 15 U.S.C. § 1127 defines "use in commerce." A trademark is "used in commerce" on goods when the trademark is in some way attached to the goods and the goods are sold or transported in commerce. "Use in commerce" on services means that the trademark is used or displayed in the sale or advertising of the services, and the services are rendered in more than one state or in the U.S. and a foreign country.

In most cases, determining whether a defendant used a mark in commerce is simple. However, courts have expanded the definition in light of recent Internet cases. For example, the first, third, eighth and ninth circuits have all held that keyword-triggered advertising is trademark use. In addition, although hidden from view to the general public, the use of trademarks in meta tags is considered "use" of a trademark for the purposes of infringement.[4] For example, in *Playboy Enterprises v. Welles*, the court found that the defendant's use of the plaintiff's trademark "Playmate" on her site as a meta tag was use of the "Playmate" trademark.[5]

Likelihood of Confusion

The likelihood of confusion requirement protects consumers and promotes informational integrity in the marketplace.[6] Generally, to be liable for trademark infringement, there must be a likelihood that the defendant's use of the trademark will cause confusion. Although evidence of actual confusion is not required, it must be probable that an appreciable number of the reasonable purchasers would be confused by the defendant's use of the trademark as to the source, sponsorship or affiliation of the associated goods or services. If no one is likely to be confused by the defendant's use of a trademark, then that use is permissible.[7]

There is no consensus on how to determine likelihood of confusion and the Supreme Court has not opined directly on the issue. To determine whether there is likelihood of confusion, almost every circuit has created a balancing test that considers a number of factors. Many of the factors are similar across circuits and no single factor is determinative. For example, factors that may be relevant to a likelihood of confusion determination include (1) the strength of the mark, (2) the proximity of the goods, (3) the similarity of the marks, (4) evidence of actual confusion, (5) the marketing channels used, (6) the type of goods and the degree of care a purchaser is likely to exercise in purchasing the goods, (7) the defendant's intent in using the mark, and (8) the likelihood of expansion of the product lines at issue.[8] These eight factors are applied in the 9th Circuit and known as the *Sleekcraft* factors.

The factors provide a useful analytical tool for courts to use. However, students should remember that courts decide the outcome of likelihood of confusion cases based on the totality of the facts.

---

[4] Meta tags are hidden information included in the code that is used to create a web page and are primarily used by search engines to catalog the contents of a particular site.

[5] Playboy Enterprises, Inc. v. Welles, 7 F. Supp. 2d 1098 (S.D. Cal.), *aff'd*, 162 F.3d 1169 (9th Cir. 1998).

[6] Groeneveld Transp. Efficiency, Inc. v. Lubecore Int'l, Inc., 730 F.3d 494, 504, 108 U.S.P.Q.2d 1022 (6th Cir. 2013).

[7] Libman Co. v. Vining Indus., Inc., 69 F.3d 1360, 1361 (7th Cir. 1995).

[8] AMF Inc. v. Sleekcraft Boats, 599 F.2d 341, 348 (9th Cir. 1979) *abrogated on other grounds by* Mattel, Inc. v. Walking Mountain Prods., 353 F.3d 792 (9th Cir. 2003).

The Strength of the Mark

The strength of a mark gauges how well it functions as a source identifier. The public associates a strong trademark with one source. A determination that the mark is weak weighs against a finding of likelihood of confusion.

The Proximity of the Goods

The more related the disputing parties' goods or services are, the more likely consumers are to be confused. Related goods are those "products which would be reasonably thought by the buying public to come from the same source if sold under the same mark."[9]

The Similarity of the Marks

Confusion may occur in many ways based on the characteristics of the marks in question. Two marks that look similar could confuse consumers. Similarly, word marks that sound the same could lead to confusion. Finally, marks that convey the same meaning to consumers could cause confusion amongst consumers. Generally, likelihood of confusion can be proven by survey evidence, evidence of actual confusion or by inferences made by comparing the marks at issue.

Evidence of Actual Confusion

If a consumer has observed the defendant's mark and believed that the defendant's product was made or sponsored by the plaintiff, then actual confusion has occurred.[10] While not determinative, evidence of actual confusion can be persuasive. For example, the simultaneous use of two marks over a long period without evidence of actual confusion suggests that there is no likelihood of confusion.[11]

The Marketing Channels Used

This factor examines the parties' advertising and trade activities. Courts may also examine if there is overlap in the customer base. Generally, the more different the advertising channels and trade channels are, the less likely it is that consumers can be confused.

---

[9] Standard Brands, Inc. v. Smidler, 151 F.2d 34, 37 (CA 2 1945).

[10] 5–5 Gilson on Trademarks § 5.04 (2017).

[11] Falcon Rice Mill, Inc. v. Community Rice Mill, Inc., 725 F.2d 336, 347 n. 13 (5th Cir.1984).

The Type of Goods and the Degree of Care a Purchaser Is Likely to Exercise in Purchasing the Goods

This factor reviews the type of goods or services the parties are providing and examines consumers' purchasing behavior. It less likely that consumers that exercise great care will be confused by a defendant's use of a mark. For example, consumers are often more educated and discriminating when making more expensive purchases.

The Defendant's Intent in Using the Mark

If a defendant intentionally used the plaintiff's mark, then most courts conclude that the defendant intended to cause confusion. In contrast, a determination that the defendant did not use the plaintiff's mark in bad faith does not indicate that there is no likelihood of confusion. A showing of bad faith is powerful but not determinative evidence of likelihood of confusion. Courts evaluate the defendant's intent in conjunction with the other factors.

The Likelihood of Expansion of the Product Lines

A trademark owner has a legitimate interest in expanding its trademark use to new products.[12] In examining this factor, courts consider whether the senior user of a mark will enter into the junior user's market category. For example, how likely is it that a trademark owner selling jewelry will enter into the defendant's cosmetic market? If it is likely that the trademark owner will expand the use of their mark, then it is more likely that consumers will be confused by the defendant's use of the mark.

Other Forms of Confusion

This section summarizes other commonly recognized forms of confusion in trademark law including reverse confusion, initial interest confusion, and post-sale confusion.

Reverse Confusion

Reverse confusion occurs when a junior user's use of a mark is so prevalent that consumers incorrectly believe that the junior user is the source of products or goods sold with the senior user's mark. Typically, in these fact scenarios, the senior user is a smaller entity and the junior user is a larger organization.

---

[12] 5–5 Gilson on Trademarks § 5.07 (2017).

Initial Interest Confusion

Initial interest confusion occurs when a defendant uses another's mark to lure consumers to its products or services. Initial interest confusion damages the trademark owner by diverting away potential business. It also damages the consumer by causing the consumer to by a different brand of goods than he was seeking. Recent initial interest confusion cases involve consumer diversion on the Internet. The requirements for showing initial interest confusion in the Internet context vary by circuit.

Post-Sale Confusion

Post-sale confusion relies on the fact that trademark infringement may occur when non-purchasers of goods are confused as to the source of goods or services. "When someone other than the purchaser of an item erroneously believes that product was made by the plaintiff, the defendant may be liable for 'post-sale confusion.' "[13] A common example of post-sale confusion happens in the counterfeiting context. For example, if Hera knowingly buys a counterfeit iPhone and her friend Joe erroneously believes that Hera's phone was made by the true manufacturer, Apple Computer, then this is an instance of post-sale confusion.

Defenses to Trademark Infringement

This section summarizes the most common defenses to trademark infringement covered in an IP survey course.

Genericness

In a suit for trademark infringement, the defendant may argue that the asserted mark is generic. As defined in Chapter 1, a generic term is understood to identify a general category of goods or services. Generic terms are not eligible for trademark protection. Evidence of a mark's genericness can include whether it is included in a dictionary and how it is used in public discourse by consumers and by the media. A word or phrase may be generic on its face, or it may become generic over time. The process for a mark that transitions from protectable to generic is called genericide. Examples of word marks that have become generic include, "elevator," "refrigerator," and "trampoline."

Functionality

A defendant in a trademark infringement lawsuit may argue that an asserted mark is functional as a defense to trademark

---

[13] 5–5 Gilson on Trademarks § 5.14 [3][a] (2017).

infringement. The functionality doctrine states that a useful product feature cannot be protected by trademark law. A product feature is functional if it is essential to the use or purpose of the product or it affects its cost and quality.[14]

If the product feature is subject to patent protection there is a strong inference that the feature is functional. For example, in *Traffix Devices v. Marketing Displays Inc.*, the Supreme Court found that a dual spring design for a road sign (that was also the subject of an expired patent) was functional and therefore not protectable as a trademark.[15] To overcome the functionality defense, the party claiming infringement must establish that the asserted mark is not functional. One way to accomplish this is to present evidence that the product feature at issue is ornamental, incidental or arbitrary.

Abandonment

Because trademark rights arise from use, the intentional lack of use of a trademark may harm or extinguish those rights. A trademark is abandoned if its owner discontinues using the trademark with no intention to resume use. Nonuse of a trademark for two consecutive years is prima facie evidence of abandonment.[16] Scenarios that commonly involve abandonment include discontinued use, unsupervised licenses, and assignment of a trademark in gross.

Unsupervised Licenses

When a licensor licenses the use of her trademark to a licensee, the licensor must exercise control over the nature and quality of the goods or services sold under the mark. Specifically, the licensor must ensure that the licensee's products are of equal quality to the products previously associated with the licensor's mark. A licensor that fails to ensure that the licensee's products are of equal quality to the products previously associated with the licensor's goods has issued a naked license, and risks abandonment of her trademark. This harsh result protects the consuming public by ensuring that the quality of goods sold under a licensed trademark is consistent.

Assignments in Gross

An assignment in gross occurs when an owner assigns trademark rights without the goodwill of the organization associated

---

[14] Inwood Labs. v. Ives Labs., 456 U.S. 844, 850 n.10, 102 S. Ct. 2182, 2187 (1982).

[15] Traffix Devices v. Mktg. Displays, 532 U.S. 23, 35, 121 S. Ct. 1255, 1263 (2001)("MDI cannot gain the exclusive right to produce sign stands using the dual-spring design by asserting that consumers associate it with the look of the invention itself.")

[16] 15 U.S.C. § 1127 (2017).

with the trademark. Examples of goodwill include tangible items or other assets that contribute to consumers' willingness to purchase the trademarked goods or services.[17] For example, if the assignor has abandoned the subject trademark and it has no goodwill, then the assignee does not obtain any rights in the mark.[18] To determine whether an assignor has transferred the goodwill of a business, a court may consider evidence that the assignor transferred tangible assets to the assignee, evidence that the product associated with the transferred trademark has not changed substantially after the transfer, and the status of the assignor after the assignment.

Fair Use

An alleged infringer of a trademark may assert that they made fair use of the trademark as a defense to infringement. The two types of fair use covered in most IP survey courses are "classic" fair use and "nominative" fair use. In addition, there are instances where an artist has asserted fair use as a defense to trademark infringement where the artist has used the trademark in an artistically relevant work.

Generally, in a "classic" fair use defense, the alleged infringer asserts that the term at issue is descriptive and that she made fair use of the mark in good faith to describe her product or service. For example, in *Zatarains, Inc. V. Oak Grove Smokehouse, Inc.*, the court held that the defendants made fair use of the term "fish fry" to describe their products and therefore did not infringe Zatarains' "Fish-Fri" mark.[19]

In contrast, nominative fair use arises when the alleged infringer uses the plaintiff's trademark to describe the plaintiff's goods or services in comparative advertising or in referential usage. A common referential use is when an entity uses another's trademark in a news story or in reviewing a product or service associated with the referenced trademark. For example, the website thewirecutter. com makes referential use of trademarks like Apple, Sonos, and Ford in its articles that review products associated with these trademarks.

The fair use defense may also arise in an artistic context. Some trademarks have expressive value because they can be used to communicate and idea. The public has an interest in free expression and the First Amendment protects the use of a mark to communicate an idea or expression. For example, using another's trademark in the title of an artistic work does not violate the Lanham Act unless (1)

---

[17] 1–3 Gilson on Trademarks § 3.06 [4] (2017).

[18] 1–3 Gilson on Trademarks § 3.06 [6] (2017).

[19] Zatarains, Inc. v. Oak Grove Smokehouse, Inc., 698 F.2d 786, 796 (5th Cir. 1983) *abrogated on other grounds by* KP Permanent Make-Up, Inc. v. Lasting Impression I, Inc., 543 U.S. 111, 125 S. Ct. 542, 160 L. Ed. 2d 440 (2004).

the title has no artistic relevance to the underlying work or (2) misleads as to the source of the content of the literary work.[20]

Generally, to successfully assert a defense of fair use, a defendant must establish that (1) the plaintiff's goods or services are not readily identifiable without use of the trademark, (2) the defendant used only as much of the mark that was reasonably necessary to identify the plaintiff's goods or services, and (3) the defendant did nothing to falsely suggest sponsorship or endorsement by the trademark holder. For example, in *New Kids on the Block v. News America Pub., Inc.*, the Ninth Circuit found that a newspaper's use of a popular boy band's name in a contest was a nominative fair use because the newspaper's use did not imply sponsorship or endorsement.[21] In contrast, in *Brother Records, Inc. v. Jardine*, the Ninth Circuit held that Al Jardine, a former member of the Beach Boys band, did not make a fair use of the Beach Boys trademark when he used it in association with his solo tour because his use implied sponsorship by the Beach Boys.[22]

Secondary Liability

A party who does not directly use a defendant's mark in commerce may still be liable for infringement under theories of contributory and indirect infringement. A party (such as a manufacturer or distributor of goods) who intentionally aids or encourages trademark infringement may be liable for contributory infringement.[23] Examples of facts that may give rise to contributory infringement liability include a party that supplies generic drugs to a manufacturer that mislabels the drugs or a party knowingly selling or facilitating the sale of counterfeit goods. In contrast, a party may be liable as an indirect infringer for producing goods with infringing trademarks and providing those goods to the infringer for resale.[24]

False Advertising

Section 43(a)(2) of the Lanham Act provides a federal cause of action for false advertising. False advertising occurs when a party misrepresents a quality about his goods and services or of another's goods or services. Specifically, a party is liable for false advertising if they use "in commerce any word, term, name symbol, or device, or any combination thereof, or any false designation of origin, false or

---

[20] Rogers v. Grimaldi, 875 F.2d 994, 999 (2d Cir. 1989).

[21] New Kids on the Block v. News Am. Publ'g, Inc., 971 F.2d 302, 309 (9th Cir. 1992).

[22] Brother Records, Inc. v. Jardine, 318 F.3d 900, 908 (9th Cir. 2003).

[23] 3–11 Gilson on Trademarks § 11.02 [1][h] (2017).

[24] Id.

misleading description of fact, or false or misleading representation of fact which" in commercial advertising or promotion, misrepresents the nature, characteristics, qualities, or geographic origin of his or another person's goods, services, or commercial activities and the plaintiff has been or is likely to be damaged by such use.[25]

A use or misrepresentation can be literally false or implicitly false. A statement is literally false when it is unambiguous and not true. For example, advertising that a jacket is made out of 100% leather when it is made out of 100% nylon is a literally false statement.

An implied falsehood is a literally true or ambiguous representation that is likely to mislead or confuse consumers. To be successful under a theory of implied falsehood, the plaintiff must show that the statement at issue is material and present evidence that the public was misled by the material statement. A statement is material if it is likely to influence a consumer's purchasing decision. Evidence that the public has been misled can come in the form of extrinsic evidence such as customer testimony, marketing surveys, and sales data.

Two common defenses to a claim of false advertising are puffing and free speech. Puffing occurs when a party makes a statement of opinion upon which no reasonable consumer would rely. For example, a moving company claiming that its movers are stronger than Hercules cannot be based on fact and therefore is not actionable.[26] Similarly, the false advertising statute cannot be used to prohibit non-commercial speech because it would violate the First Amendment right to free speech. Thus, a party must make a false or misleading statement in a commercial context to be liable for false advertising under § 43(a).[27]

Dilution

Section 43(c) of the Lanham Act provides for a federal cause of action for dilution. A cause of action for dilution provides owners of famous trademarks with an additional way to protect property interests in their marks. Specifically, dilution only applies to famous marks that are inherently distinctive or have acquired secondary meaning.

In analyzing a dilution cause of action, the focus is on the junior user's goods. Generally, a successful claim for dilution establishes that (1) the plaintiff owns a famous mark, (2) the defendant has used

---

[25] 15 U.S.C. § 1125 (2017).

[26] Radio Today, Inc. v. Westwood One, Inc., 684 F. Supp. 68, 74 (S.D.N.Y. 1988).

[27] 2–7 Gilson on Trademarks § 7.02 [3] (2017).

a diluting mark in commerce, (3) the similarity between the famous mark and the junior user's mark gives rise to an association between the two marks and (4) that association impairs the distinctiveness or harms the reputation of a famous mark. Section 43(c)(2)(A) of the Lanham Act defines a famous mark as one that is "widely recognized by the general consuming public of the United States as a designation of source of the goods or services of the mark's owner."[28] To determine whether a mark is famous, courts consider evidence related to the amount and geographic reach of advertising and publicity of the mark, the volume and geographic scope of the sales of goods and services related to the mark, and the extent of actual recognition of the mark.

Notably, a successful case for dilution does not require evidence of likelihood of confusion. Instead, a plaintiff must prove there is actual dilution or a likelihood of dilution. Accordingly, extrinsic evidence such as survey results about how the asserted and alleged infringing marks are used in commerce is critical to a successful dilution claim.

There are two types of dilution IP survey students should be familiar with—blurring and tarnishment. First, tarnishment is the unauthorized use of a mark on products or services that are of lower quality or unsavory as compared to the authorized goods. For example, a court has held that a defendant's use of the term "Victor's Little Secret" in association with an adult toy store tarnished the "Victoria's Secret" trademark.[29]

Second, blurring is the use of a designation or mark that (1) creates a likelihood of association arising from the similarity between the challenged designation and the plaintiff's mark that is likely to (2) impair the distinctiveness of the plaintiff's mark.[30] Blurring occurs when an owner's famous mark is being used on unassociated or far removed goods and the ordinary consumer makes an association with the famous mark. For example, if a junior user uses the mark "FORD" on laptop computers then it is likely that this use will impair the distinctiveness of the Ford Motor Company's "FORD" trademark. In a successful cause of action for blurring, the plaintiff must show that after the mark became famous, the defendant used the challenged designation in interstate commerce as a trademark or trade name. Finally, the plaintiff must show that the defendant's use

---

[28] 35 U.S.C. § 1125 (c)(2)(A).

[29] V Secret Catalogue, Inc. v. Moseley, 605 F.3d 382, 385, 95 U.S.P.Q.2d 1050 (6th Cir. 2010).

[30] Note that the similarity between the challenged designation and the plaintiff's trademark need not be substantial. *See* Tiffany (NJ) Inc. v. eBay, Inc. 600 F.3d 93, 111 n. 18 (2d Cir. 2010).

is likely to cause blurring by creating a likelihood of association arising from the similarity of the marks from the standpoint of the ordinary consuming public of the U.S. that is likely to impair the distinctiveness of the plaintiff's mark.

Section 43(c)(3) of the Lanham Act specifies three exceptions to a claim of liability for dilution: (1) fair use, (2) all forms of news reporting and news commentary, and (3) any noncommercial use of the mark. Accordingly, "the use of famous marks in non-commercial settings, such as parodies, consumer product reviews, and news and investigative reports, would not be actionable."[31] For example, in *Louis Vuitton Malletier S.A. v. Haute Diggity Dog, LLC*, the defendant, Haute Diggity Dog, sold chew toys that parodied luxury brands such as Louis Vuitton. Louis Vuitton asserted that Haute Diggity Dog's products diluted its brand on blurring and tarnishment grounds. In their defense, Haute Diggity Dog successfully asserted that their products parodied Louis Vuitton's products and therefore made a fair use of the Louis Vuitton mark.[32]

Trademarks and the Internet

This section briefly summarizes legal issues regarding trademarks and the Internet.

Domain Names

Domain names are used to identify web pages with particular Internet protocol addresses. Domain names can become valid trademarks. In turn, domain names may also infringe existing trademarks. Because domain names are unique, parties may dispute the ownership rights of a desirable domain name.

As an alternative to litigation, the Uniform Dispute Resolution Policy ("UDRP") is implemented by the Internet Corporation for Assigned Names and Numbers ("ICANN") as an administrative process to address domain name disputes. While the UDRP process does not preclude a separate legal action, it does provide a streamlined administrative process. A party may file a UDRP complaint against another party over the registration or use of a disputed domain name. The complainant must establish that (1) the disputed domain name is identical or confusingly similar, (2) the domain holder has no legitimate rights or interest in the domain, and (3) the domain was registered in bad faith. The domain holder has twenty days to respond to a complaint and then a panel of experts issues their decision within 14 days of the domain owner's response.

---

[31] 2–5A Gilson on Trademarks § 5A.01 [b] (2017).

[32] Louis Vuitton Malletier S.A. v. Haute Diggity Dog, LLC, 507 F.3d 252, 256 (4th Cir. 2007).

If the complainant is successful, his remedies could include the transfer of the disputed domain name to him or cancellation of the domain.

Cybersquatting

The Anti Cybersquatting Piracy Act provides for a federal cause of action for cybersquatting.[33] This provision prevents a person from using a trademark in a domain name just to entice the mark owner to buy the site. To be successful in a cause of action for cybersquatting the plaintiff must show that they own a valid trademark that is distinctive or famous. Next, that the complained of domain name is identical or confusingly similar to the plaintiff's trademark. Finally, the plaintiff must demonstrate that the defendant registered the disputed domain name in bad faith.

For example, the organization People for the Ethical Treatment of Animals ("PETA") sued Michael Doughney under the ACPA after he registered and maintained PETA.org as a site that promoted "People Eating Tasty Animals." PETA successfully argued that the defendant established the site in bad faith. In doing so, it relied on evidence that the defendant used false statements to register the site, that the defendant intended to confuse the public, and that the defendant suggested that PETA settle with him several times.[34]

Counterfeiting

Counterfeiting is the intentional copying of a trademark that usually involves the manufacture and distribution of goods under another's mark without their permission. Counterfeiting is punishable as a crime. It is a felony to knowingly use a counterfeit mark in connection with the sale of goods or services. Sections 34(b) and 36 of the Lanham Act also provide for the seizure of counterfeit goods and the destruction of infringing articles respectively.

It is a common misconception that counterfeiting is a victimless crime. The proliferation of counterfeit goods may tarnish a well-respected brand. In addition, there is evidence that criminal and terrorist organizations use the sale of counterfeit goods to fund their activities. Further, the sale of counterfeit goods such as medicine, baby formula, and machine parts pose significant health and safety risks to the public.[35] Finally, there is evidence that some counterfeit

---

[33] 15 U.S.C. § 1125(d) (2017).

[34] People for the Ethical Treatment of Animals v. Doughney, 263 F.3d 359, 369 (4th Cir. 2001).

[35] *Substandard, spurious, falsely labelled, falsified and counterfeit (SFFC) medical products*, World Health Organization Fact Sheet, Updated January 2016.

goods are made in factories that exploit their workers by paying them low wages in unsafe conditions.

Remedies

Two basic remedies available for trademark infringement are injunctive relief and damages.

Injunctive Relief

Injunctive relief may be in the form of a preliminary injunction or a permanent injunction. At its discretion, a court may also tailor injunctive relief to suit the facts of a particular case. These qualified injunctions include relief such as disclaimers, modification to logos, and setting geographic limitations on the use of marks. For example, in *AMF Inc., v. Sleekcraft Boats*, the court suggested that the defendant's logo be used in conjunction with the Sleekcraft name on advertising and promotional materials.[36] Corrective advertising is another form of injunctive relief. Finally, a court may cancel trademark registrations or order that infringing articles be destroyed.

Damages

The damages remedy for trademark infringement can include the recovery of the defendant's profits, other money damages, and attorney fees. To obtain a defendant's profits, the plaintiff must show that the infringement was willful and deliberate, i.e., that the defendant was attempting to gain the value of an established name of the plaintiff.[37] An award of money damages may be supported by evidence of the plaintiff's direct injury and lost profits. In some instances, a plaintiff may also recover damages in the amount of the defendant's profits under an unjust enrichment theory. Finally, a party may recover attorney fees upon a finding that the defendant's conduct was willful or deliberate.

---

[36] AMF Inc. v. Sleekcraft Boats, 599 F.2d 341, 355 (9th Cir. 1979) *abrogated on other grounds by* Mattel, Inc. v. Walking Mountain Prods., 353 F.3d 792 (9th Cir. 2003).

[37] *See* 15 U.S.C. § 1114(1)(b) (2017).

TRADEMARK INFRINGEMENT CHECKLIST

With the above Review in mind, the Trademark Infringement Checklist is presented below.

A. **DETERMINE IF THE PLAINTIFF OWNS RIGHTS IN A VALID TRADEMARK.** Is the asserted trademark valid?

     1. **Subject Matter.** Is the mark protectable subject matter? Review the summary of trade secret subject matter in Chapter 1.

     2. **Rights and Federal Registration.** Has the plaintiff used the allegedly infringed mark in commerce? Does the owner have priority in the mark? Is the allegedly infringed trademark registered on the Principal Register? Review Chapter 2 for a summary of the law on obtaining trademark rights.

B. **DETERMINE IF THE TRADEMARK WAS USED IN COMMERCE.** Has the defendant used the trademark in commerce in association with a good or service that was sold or advertised to the public? Remember that courts have held that the use of a trademark in keyword advertising and in meta tags can be a use in commerce.

C. **DETERMINE IF THERE IS LIKELIHOOD OF CONFUSION.** Determine if the alleged infringer's use of the mark created a likelihood of confusion.

     1. **"Likelihood."** Remember that evidence of actual confusion is not required. However, it must be probable that an appreciable number of the reasonable purchasers would be confused by the defendant's use of the mark as to the source, sponsorship or affiliation of the associated goods or services.

     2. **Likelihood of Confusion Factors.** Evaluate the factors applied in the relevant circuit for likelihood of confusion. Remember, that no one factor is determinative. The 9th Circuit applies the *Sleekcraft* factors, summarized below.

         a. **Strength of the Mark.** The strength of a mark gauges how well it functions as a source identifier.

         b. **The Proximity of the Goods.** How related are the parties' goods or services? The more related the goods and services are the more likely that consumers are to be confused.

c. **The Similarity of the Marks.** Are the marks similar visually, sonically or in meaning? The more similar the marks, the more likely they are to cause confusion.

d. **Evidence of Actual Confusion.** Is there evidence that consumers were actually confused by the defendant's use of the alleged infringing mark? While not determinative, evidence of actual confusion is persuasive evidence that there is a likelihood of confusion.

e. **Marketing Channels.** What is the nature of the parties' advertising and trade activities? Are their products advertised in the same magazines or sold in the same stores? The more similar the parties' advertising and trade channels, the more likely there is to be confusion amongst consumers.

f. **Types of Goods and Degree of Purchaser Care.** Are the goods or services at issue expensive luxury items or inexpensive commodities? How much research and care do consumers of the products or services at issue expend before making a buying decision? The more careful consumers are about a purchasing decision, the less likely it is that they will be confused.

g. **Defendant's Intent.** Did the defendant intentionally use the plaintiff's trademark? If so, this factor weighs in favor of a finding of likelihood of confusion.

h. **Likelihood of Expansion of Product Lines.** How likely is it that the trademark owner will expand the use of her trademark to new products in the junior user's market category? If the trademark owner will expand the use of their mark, then it is more likely that consumers will be confused by the defendant's use of the mark.

D. **DEFENSES TO TRADEMARK INFRINGEMENT.** Consider the available defenses to trademark infringement.

1. **Genericness.** Generic terms are not eligible for trademark protection. Generic terms identify a general category of goods or services. A once valid trademark may become generic over time. Genericide occurs when a mark transitions from protectable to generic.

2. **Functionality.** Is the asserted mark functional? A functional feature cannot be protected as a trademark. A feature is functional if it is essential to the use or purpose

of a product or if it affects product cost or quality. There is a strong inference that patented features are functional.

3. **Abandonment.** Has the trademark owner used the mark in commerce? An owner abandons his trademark if he discontinues using the trademark with no intention to resume use. Nonuse of a trademark for two consecutive years is prima facie evidence of abandonment.

   a. **Unsupervised Licensing.** Has the trademark been licensed to a third party? Naked licensing of a trademark can result in abandonment of a trademark. A licensor that licenses its trademark to a licensee but fails to ensure that the licensee's products associated with the licensed trademark are of equal quality to the products previously associated with the licensor's goods is deemed to have issued a naked license.

   b. **Assignment in gross.** A defendant may challenge the validity of an asserted mark on grounds that the mark was assigned in gross. Did the owner of the mark assign its rights to a third party without transferring the goodwill of the enterprise associated with the mark?

5. **Fair use.** In defense of a trademark infringement claim, a defendant may assert that he made a fair use of an asserted trademark. The good faith use of a descriptive mark to describe a defendant's own products and not as a trademark, can be a fair use of a trademark. In addition, using a plaintiff's trademark to describe the plaintiff's goods or services is a fair use of the plaintiff's trademark. Further, the use of a trademark in the expression of ideas may be protected by the First Amendment unless it has no artistic relevance to the underlying work or misleads the public as to the source of the content of the expression.

E. **FALSE ADVERTISING.** Determine whether a party has misrepresented the qualities of his goods or services or another's goods or services. The nature of a misrepresentation can be literally false or implicitly false.

1. **Literally False.** Assess the statement(s) made by the accused party. Are the statements false and unambiguous? If so, the statement can be characterized as literally false and a misrepresentation.

2. **Implied Falsehood.** Implicitly false statements are true or ambiguous statements that are likely to mislead

consumers. However, to be actionable, there must be evidence that the statements were material. A statement is material if a consumer's decision to purchase a good or service was influenced by the complained of statement.

3. **Defenses to a Claim of False Advertising.** Consider the available defenses to false advertising. Would a reasonable consumer rely on the accused statement to make a purchasing decision? If not, the accused statement may be puffery. In addition, consider the context in which the statement was made. If the statement was non-commercial in nature, it might be protected as free speech under the First Amendment.

F. **DILUTION.** Determine whether the use of a mark by a junior user impairs the distinctiveness or harms the reputation of a senior user's mark. Generally, a successful claim for dilution establishes that (1) the plaintiff owns a famous mark, (2) the defendant has used a diluting mark in commerce, (3) the similarity between the famous mark and the junior user's mark gives rise to an association between the two marks and (4) that association impairs the distinctiveness or harms the reputation of a famous mark.

1. **Famous Marks.** In order to be successful in a cause of action for dilution, the senior user's mark must be famous. A famous mark is widely recognized in the U.S. by the consuming public as a designation of the source of the goods or services of the mark's owner.

2. **Tarnishment.** Consider the products or services that were subject to unauthorized use of the mark. Compare them to the products or services of the senior user of the mark. Tarnishment occurs if the unauthorized use of the mark occurred on products that are of lower quality or are unsavory as compared to the senior user's products or services.

3. **Blurring.** Consider the products or services that were subject to unauthorized use of the mark. Compare them to the senior user's products or services. Blurring occurs if the senior user's mark is being used on unassociated or far removed goods and the ordinary consumer makes an association with the famous mark.

4. **Exceptions to a Claim of Dilution.** Examine the context in which the famous mark is being used. Fair use of a famous mark, use of a famous mark in news reporting, or

use of a famous mark in a non-commercial setting are not actionable.

G. **EVALUATE THE REMEDIES AVAILABLE FOR THE ACCUSED HARM.** Two basic remedies available for trademark infringement are injunctive relief and damages.

    1. **Injunctive Relief.** A court has many different options concerning injunctive relief. The type of injunctive relief a court grants depends on the specific facts of the case. Courts use qualified injunctive relief to prevent further harm to the plaintiff, protect consumers and promote healthy competition in the marketplace. In some cases, a court may cancel a trademark registration or order that infringing articles be destroyed.

    2. **Damages.** The damages remedy for trademark infringement can include the recovery of the defendant's profits, other money damages and attorney fees.

ILLUSTRATIVE PROBLEMS

Here are two problems that illustrate how the Checklist can be used to resolve trademark infringement questions.

■   **PROBLEM 3.1**   ■

Recall the facts from problem 2.1.

App Amazing is one of the best-selling brands of apple juice in the Unites States. Since 2002, more than 500 million bottles of App Amazing have been sold. App Amazing markets its products in the U.S. and foreign countries under a family of trademarks that include the term "APP." App Amazing's trademark, "APP," was registered on the Principal Register by the USPTO on September 22, 2002, for use with fruit juices.

App Amazing contends it designed its mark to be distinctive and act as a source-identifier. It has invested millions of dollars in the marketing and sale of products under the APP brand. App Amazing asserts that the public associates the APP brand with quality fruit products. The mark "APP" became incontestable in 2007.

Hubert Goddard, d/b/a Appl Beverages ("APPL"), sells a line of apple-flavored energy drinks and snacks. APPL began selling it apple-flavored products labeled "app" in April 2013. App Amazing learned of APPL's activities and informed Goddard of App Amazing's ownership interest in the "APP" brand trademarks. When Goddard refused to change its packaging, App Amazing filed suit, alleging that

APPL's use of the word "app" violated App Amazing's trademark rights under the Lanham Act.

Discuss App Amazing's argument that consumers will be confused by Goddard's use of the mark "app."

Analysis

In a trademark infringement suit, the plaintiff must prove that it has a protectable interest in the mark and that the defendant's use of the mark is likely to cause consumer confusion. Here, the question asks you to address the issue of likelihood of confusion.

App Amazing must show that a reasonably prudent consumer is likely to be confused by the use of APPL's "app" on its products. For example, do consumers associate App Amazing with APPL's products marked with "app?" Students should apply the *Sleekcraft* factors to the facts, or other factors if they studied different factors from another circuit.

Strength of the Mark

The strength of a mark gauges how well it functions as a source identifier. On the distinctiveness spectrum, the "APP" mark is suggestive. Therefore, it is entitled to greater protection than descriptive marks. In addition, given its marketing efforts, the facts indicate that "APP" has marketplace recognition and is commercially strong. Thus, this factor weighs in App Amazing's favor.

The Proximity of the Goods

The more related the disputing parties' goods or services are, the more likely consumers are to be confused. Here, App Amazing's apple juice is related to APPL's energy drinks. They are both beverages that a consumer might reasonably associate with one another and be confused by. Accordingly, this factor also weighs in App Amazing's favor.

The Similarity of the Marks

Similar marks are likely to cause confusion. Marks may be similar in appearance, sound or meaning. Here, the marks are almost identical except for the case of text. App Amazing uses all caps— "APP." APPL uses the same letters in lowercase. Each mark sounds the same and is intended to convey the same meaning—that the beverage contains apple as an ingredient. Thus, the similarity of the marks weighs in favor of App Amazing.

Evidence of Actual Confusion

If a consumer has observed the defendant's mark and believed that the defendant's product was made or sponsored by the plaintiff, then actual confusion has occurred. Here, the facts fail to provide any evidence of actual confusion. Thus, this factor does not weigh in favor of either party.

The Marketing Channels Used

Similar or convergent marketing channels increase the likelihood of confusion. Here, the parties likely sell their products in the same cities, to the same stores, and customers. In addition, other products are marketed to similar consumers. Thus, the marketing channel factor weighs in App Amazing's favor.

The Type of Goods and Purchaser Degree of Care

This factor reviews the type of goods or services the parties are providing and examines consumers' purchasing behavior. As established above, the parties' products are similar. Because the parties' products are inexpensive beverages it is more likely that they will be confused because purchasers generally exercise less care when buying goods of this nature. Thus, this factor also weighs in favor of App Amazing.

The Defendant's Intent and Likelihood of Expansion of the Product Lines

If a defendant intentionally used the plaintiff's mark, then most courts conclude that the defendant intended to cause confusion. In examining the likelihood of expansion factor, courts generally consider whether the senior user of a mark will enter into the junior user's market category. Here, the facts fail to provide any evidence of intent or likelihood of expansion. Thus, this factor does not weigh in favor of either party.

Totality of the Facts

Based on the above analysis, the totality of the facts seem to weigh in favor of App Amazing's contention that APPL's use of the "app" mark is likely to cause confusion.

■ PROBLEM 3.2 ■

Potato Factory manufactures potato chips and distributes them in packaging with "SMOKY 'Tato Chips" displayed prominently on the front. Potato Factory obtained federal registration for the mark "SMOKY 'Tato Chips" in 2000. The SMOKY trademark is well recognized by consumers and has become famous and distinct.

Smokeless Tobacco ("Smokeless") manufactures chewing tobacco. Smokeless sells several different types of flavored chewing tobacco labeled as barbecue, cheddar & sour cream, and classic. In 2013, desiring to simulate smoking a cigar, Smokeless launched a new flavor of chewing tobacco that was manufactured and sold in packaging labeled as "Chewing Tobacco with smoky flavor."

In 2014, sales of Potato Factory "SMOKY 'Tato Chips" drops dramatically. Potato Factory hires a consulting firm to investigate the drop in sales. After months of investigation, the firm provides a report to Potato Factory. The report contains substantial survey evidence that the drop in sales is due to customers refraining from buying "SMOKY 'Tato Chips" because they no longer like the taste.

In 2015, Potato Factory files a complaint against Smokeless for trademark dilution by blurring and tarnishment.

Discuss whether Potato Factory's claims are supported by the evidence. Also, discuss Smokeless' possible fair use defense.

Analysis

Generally, a successful claim for dilution establishes that (1) the plaintiff owns a famous mark, (2) the defendant has used a diluting mark in commerce, (3) the similarity between the famous mark and the junior user's mark gives rise to an association between the two marks and (4) that association impairs the distinctiveness or harms the reputation of a famous mark.

Blurring

Based on the facts, the analysis of first three elements of the dilution analysis is straightforward. Accordingly, students should focus on whether Smokeless' use of "smoky" impairs the distinctiveness of the "SMOKY 'Tato Chips" mark.

The facts indicate that Potato Factory's mark is famous and distinct. Potato Factory and Smokeless use the same word "smoky." However, Smokeless used the term "smoky" to describe an attribute of their product. There is no evidence that Smokeless intended for its product to be associated with Potato Factory's chips. Finally, the consultant investigation fails to provide any evidence that consumers associated "SMOKY 'Tato Chips" with Smokeless' smoky flavored chewing tobacco. Accordingly, the evidence is unlikely to support a claim for dilution by blurring.

Tarnishment

To succeed in a claim for dilution by tarnishment, Potato Factory must establish that Smokeless' use of "SMOKY Chewing Tobacco" harms the reputation of the "SMOKY 'Tato Chips" mark. Here, the survey evidence reveals that Potato Factory's drop in sales is due to customers no longer liking the taste of "SMOKY 'Tato Chips." There is no evidence that Smokeless' use of the label "Chewing Tobacco with smoky flavor" on its packaging hurt the sales of "SMOKY 'Tato Chips" or its reputation in the mind of consumers. Thus, the evidence would also fail to support Potato Factory's claim of tarnishment.

Smokeless' Fair Use Defense

Smokeless may also assert a defense of fair use. Specifically, smokeless may argue that it made a classic fair use of the descriptive term "smoky" to describe a characteristic of its product. The fair use defense requires proof of three elements: (1) the term or phrase is used only describe defendant's products; (2) the defendant did not use the mark as a trademark; and (3) the use was made in good faith. Here, the term "smoky" is used as an adjective to describe the flavor of the tobacco. There is no evidence that Smokeless attempted to use "smoky" as a trademark. Also, the facts indicate that Smokeless' new flavor was intended to simulate the flavor of smoking a cigar. This evidence supports a claim that "smoky" was used in good faith. In sum, the evidence would support an argument by Smokeless that it made a fair use of the term "smoky."

POINTS TO REMEMBER

- Whether a junior user's use of a mark will cause a likelihood of confusion with the senior user's mark is central to the analysis of most trademark infringement claims. Most circuits employ a multiple factor balancing tests to determine whether there is a likelihood of confusion. Be sure to ask your professor what balancing test, if any, they expect you to understand and apply.

- "Remember that to obtain relief in a trademark infringement case, the plaintiff must show that confusion is only likely, not that it is possible, actual or inevitable."[38]

- Under a classic fair use defense, a user of a trademark has no liability for infringement if the term is used in good faith to describe his goods or services and not as a trademark.

- To be successful in a cause of action for dilution, the senior user's mark must be famous. A famous mark is widely recognized.

- Counterfeiting is the intentional copying of a trademark. It is a felony to knowingly use a counterfeit mark in connection with the sale of goods or services.

---

[38] 5–5 Gilson on Trademarks § 5.01[1] (2017).

CHAPTER 4

Patentable Subject Matter

This chapter discusses patentable subject matter. In a typical IP course, the question of what subject matter is eligible for patenting is a student's first exposure to patent law. At first, the topic may seem straightforward. But, the courts' interpretation of the statute governing patentability, 35 U.S.C. § 101, is nuanced and continues to evolve as new technological advances are made. The Supreme Court has addressed the question of what types of inventions are patentable several times in the last decade.

On an IP exam, your professor could ask you to determine whether a certain invention would be patentable and why. This chapter summarizes the law for patentable subject matter in a way that will allow you to systematically apply the rules to most exam questions. Students should remember that although a patent document has many sections, the claims (a numbered description of the invention at the end of the patent) define the invention. Thus, the focus of any patent analysis is on the language used in the claims to describe the invention.

PATENTABLE SUBJECT MATTER REVIEW

Overview

There are three general types of patents—utility, plant and design patents. Design patents protect any new and ornamental designs of useful articles such as cookware or furniture. Plant patents protect new and distinct plant varieties. Utility patents are the most common type of patent and are the focus of this chapter.

Utility Patents

Generally, a new and useful process or product is eligible for patent protection. Section 101 of the patent act sets forth four categories of subject matter that are patent-eligible. These categories are any (1) process, (2) machine, (3) manufacture, or (4) composition of matter.[1] Patent professionals often group the last three categories

---

[1] 35 U.S.C. § 101.

under the generic umbrella of product inventions to separate them from process inventions.

Distinguishing between product and process claims is relatively easy. However, students often have difficulty categorizing product inventions as machines, manufactures or compositions of matter. Therefore, it is important to keep a simple definition and example of each category in mind.

Machine

Machines are probably the most recognizable category of patent-eligible product inventions. A machine is any mechanical apparatus. A machine may be as simple as a bottle opener or as complex as an automobile. One characteristic that may help students distinguish machines from other product inventions is that a machine is generally made up of several parts.

Manufactures and Compositions of Matter

Manufactures and compositions of matter include a broad range of things made by man.

A composition of matter is a substance formed from the combination of two or more other substances. A new chemical compound formed from an intermixture of ingredients is an example of a composition of matter. In addition, synthetically created DNA qualifies as a composition of matter and is patent eligible.

A manufacture is an article created from raw materials. Ceramics are an example of an article of manufacture. Further, manufactures serve as a catch-all category that covers items that do not readily fall into one of the other product categories.

In some instances, an invention may fall into both categories. For example, the Supreme Court has held that genetically altered living organisms are manufactures or compositions of matter.[2]

Students should be careful to distinguish man-made manufactures and compositions of matter from those that man simply discovered. Discoveries of found items, such as a naturally occurring element or other natural phenomena are not patent-eligible.

Process

A process is a method or procedure for how to do something. For example, the steps for how to make a certain chemical might be

---

[2] Diamond v. Chakrabarty, 447 U.S. 303, 307 (1980).

eligible for patent protection. In addition, a new use for a known material is eligible for patenting.

When analyzing a process invention, students should consider whether the claimed process is simply applying an abstract idea. For example, process claims directed to business methods (methods of carrying out business functions such as ordering a book online) or that use algorithms are scrutinized closely because abstract concepts are not patent-eligible. The following section summarizes the categories of subject matter that are not eligible for patenting, including abstract ideas.

Judicial Exceptions

Three judicially recognized categories are generally not eligible for patenting—(1) laws of nature, (2) natural phenomenon and (3) abstract ideas. A rationale for these exceptions is that these categories are the basic building blocks of scientific work. Thus, granting a patent in any one of these areas could preempt a scientific approach that would stifle innovation. Students should understand what types of subject matter fall into these categories and know examples of each.

Laws of Nature

Fundamental scientific principles are not eligible for patenting. In *Mayo Collaborative Servs. v. Prometheus Labs., Inc.*, the Supreme Court held that an invention claiming the relation between the characteristics of a patient's blood and the efficacy of that drug in the patient was a law of nature and therefore not patentable.[3] Einstein's law of relativity ($E=mc^2$) or Newton's law of gravity are also examples of laws of nature.

Natural Phenomenon

Things that can be found in nature are not patent-eligible. For example, a new mineral discovered in the soil or a naturally occurring segment of DNA is not patent-eligible. Even a brilliant discovery does not by itself satisfy § 101.[4]

Abstract Ideas

Ideas are not patentable. Examples of abstract ideas include basic algorithms, principal concepts and fundamental practices. One historical rationale for preventing the patenting of abstract ideas is that patents were intended to cover devices and things. Another

---

[3] Mayo Collaborative Servs. v. Prometheus Labs., Inc., 566 U.S. 66, 92 (2012).

[4] *See e.g.,* Ass'n for Molecular Pathology v. Myriad Genetics, Inc., 569 U.S. 576 (2013).

rationale is that allowing patent protection of abstract ideas would stifle innovation because inventors could prevent others from using essential concepts.

Patent claims that simply recite an abstract idea are not patent eligible. For example, the Supreme Court has held that a process claim embodying an algorithm for converting binary coded decimal numbers into pure binary numbers was patent ineligible.[5] Similarly, the Supreme Court held that a process claim on the basic concept of hedging against risk in a financial transaction was patent ineligible because the claim was attempting to cover a fundamental economic practice.[6]

When analyzing exam questions, students should keep the examples of patent-ineligible subject matter above in mind. They provide useful signposts to help analyze other questions regarding patent eligibility. However, categorizing subject matter as falling into one of the judicial exceptions does not end the patent eligibility inquiry. Under current U.S. law, a patent claim incorporating an abstract concept may still be eligible for patenting.

The Mayo Patent Eligibility Framework: Analyzing Attempts to Patent Ineligible Subject Matter

Patentability questions commonly arise in the biomedical field and with respect to software and business method patents. For example, a patent examiner may argue that a claimed software invention is nothing but an abstract idea and therefore not patentable. The Supreme Court established a two-step framework for determining whether an invention is patent eligible in *Mayo*.[7]

First, determine whether the claim in question incorporates a natural law or abstract idea. Second, if a patent claim includes natural laws or abstract ideas, evaluate whether the claim contains an inventive concept that transforms it into a patentable application. Is the invention in question applying an abstract concept to a new and useful end or integrating basic building blocks into something more? With respect to natural phenomena, a key question is did the inventor simply discover the subject matter or did she develop it?

Natural Phenomena

Things found in nature are not eligible for patenting. However, naturally occurring things that have been modified or created by man are considered manufactures or compositions of matter and are

---

[5] Gottschalk v. Benson, 409 U.S. 63, 971 (1972).

[6] Bilski v. Kappos, 561 U.S. 593, 612 (2010).

[7] Mayo Collaborative Servs. v. Prometheus Labs., Inc., 566 U.S. 66, 72 (2012).

therefore patent eligible. For example, bacteria that have been genetically modified such that the modified bacteria possess characteristics not normally found in their natural state are patentable.[8] Further, the Supreme Court has held that synthetically created DNA is patent eligible.[9]

Laws of Nature and Abstract Ideas

An invention that applies a law of nature or abstract idea to a new and useful end or integrates these basic concepts to create something more than just the abstract concept may be eligible for patenting. Accordingly, the student must next determine whether the claim contains an "inventive concept" sufficient to transform the abstract concept into a patent-eligible application.[10] But, the invention must do more than just apply the abstract concept. Simply applying an abstract concept or using a generic computer to apply the abstract concept will not qualify as an inventive concept. Instead, the claim must contain additional features that ensure that the invention is more than an attempt to just patent the abstract concept.

For example, the Supreme Court held in *Diehr* that a computer-implemented process that used a well-known mathematical equation to solve a technological problem in the rubber curing process was patent eligible.[11] In a later decision, the Supreme Court explained that the claims in *Diehr* were patent eligible because they contained additional steps that transformed the process into an inventive application of the equation.[12] Specifically, the steps of (1) obtaining constant temperature measurements inside a rubber mold and (2) repeatedly recalculating the remaining cure time by using the equation transformed the process into an inventive application of the equation.

The chart below is a basic summary of patent eligible subject matter. On an IP exam, students may be asked to apply the *Mayo* patent eligibility framework to inventions that fall in the third column.

---

[8] Diamond v. Chakrabarty, 447 U.S. 303, 309 (1980).

[9] Ass'n for Molecular Pathology v. Myriad Genetics, Inc., 569 U.S. 595 (2013) (explaining that cDNA created by a lab technician is not a product of nature and therefore patent eligible).

[10] Mayo Collaborative Servs. v. Prometheus Labs., Inc., 566 U.S. 66, 72 (2012).

[11] Diamond v. Diehr, 450 U.S. 175 (1981).

[12] Bilski v. Kappos, 561 U.S. 593, 611 (2010).

Patent Subject Matter Summary Chart

Patent Eligible	Patent Ineligible	Controversial, but Patent Eligible
Process	Laws of Nature	Software
Machine	Natural Phenomenon	Business Methods
Manufacture	Abstract ideas	Biological material
Composition of matter		

PATENTABLE SUBJECT MATTER CHECKLIST

With the above Review in mind, the Patentable Subject Matter Checklist is presented below.

A. CLASSIFY THE SUBJECT MATTER. Analyze the patent claim. Is the purported invention a product or a process?

    1. Products. Is the invention a thing made by man? Patent professionals generally refer to machines, manufactures and compositions of matter as product inventions.

        a. Machines. Is the invention an apparatus that has more than one part? E.g., a can opener or a bicycle.

        b. Compositions of Matter. Is the invention a substance created from integrating two or more ingredients? E.g., a chemical compound or genetically modified organisms.

        c. Manufactures. Is the invention an article created from raw materials? Does the invention not fit squarely into the machine or composition of matter category? E.g., a ceramic cutting board.

    2. Processes. Is the invention one or more steps for how to do something or make a thing? E.g., a series of steps for creating a chemical solution or building an apparatus.

B. DETERMINE WHETHER THE PATENT CLAIM IS DIRECTED TO PATENT ELIGIBLE SUBJECT MATTER

1. **Patent Eligible Subject Matter.** Does the subject matter of the patent claim fall squarely into the machine, composition of matter, manufacture or process category described in section A?

2. **Patent Ineligible Subject Matter.** Is the claim directed to patent-ineligible subject matter or does it involve an abstract concept?

   a. **Laws of Nature.** Is the claim directed to a fundamental scientific principle? E.g., the laws of motion or the law of gravity.

   b. **Natural Phenomena.** Is the claim directed to natural phenomena? E.g., lightning or a new mineral discovered in the earth.

   c. **Abstract Ideas.** Does the claim involve an abstract idea? For example, is the claim a process that uses a basic algorithm or a fundamental practice? E.g., a mathematical formula or an understood economic principle.

C. DETERMINE WHETHER A CLAIM INVOLVING AN ABSTRACT CONCEPT IS STILL PATENT ELIGIBLE. There is a two-step test for distinguishing inventions that claim laws of nature, natural phenomena and abstract ideas from inventions that claim patent eligible applications of those concepts.

1. **Step One.** Determine whether the claim at issue integrates a patent-ineligible concept. Does the claim use or include a law of nature, natural phenomena or abstract idea?

2. **Step Two.** If the claim involves a patent-ineligible category, does the claim contain an inventive concept?

   a. **Additional Features.** Does the claim include additional features (steps or elements)? Are the additional features well known (e.g., a generic computer)?

   b. **Determine Whether the Additional Features Transform the Patent Ineligible Subject Matter into a Patent-Eligible Application.** Do the additional features transform the claim into an inventive application of an abstract concept?

3.   **Review Policy Reasons for Why or Why Not the Claim at Issue Should Be Patent Eligible.** Does the claim cover a fundamental principle? Will granting a patent foreclose others from using basic tools of scientific or technological work?

ILLUSTRATIVE PROBLEMS

Here are two problems that illustrate how the Checklist can be used to resolve patent subject matter questions.

■   PROBLEM 4.1   ■

A patent applicant seeks to patent a process for improving the application of air to a furnace. It is generally known that pumping air into a furnace using a blowing apparatus causes the temperature of the furnace to rise. Further, scientists have discovered that warm air is better than cold air at increasing furnace temperatures. This technique is considered a fundamental principle in the furnace industry.

The claimed process requires that cold air produced by the blowing apparatus be passed into an intermediate receptacle. The receptacle is artificially heated to a high temperature by an external device. A pipe then transfers the heated air into the furnace.

Is the invention eligible for patenting? Briefly explain the reasoning for your decision.

Analysis

To analyze this problem, first identify what the inventor is seeking to patent. Here, the facts say that the applicant is claiming a process for improving application of air to a furnace. Accordingly, the invention seems to be a process and therefore statutory subject matter.

However, the facts also say that the act of pumping air into a furnace to increase the temperature is well known. Further, we are told that scientist understand that warm air functions better than cold air for this purpose. These facts raise a question of whether the process claim is simply directed to an abstract idea and therefore patent-ineligible. To answer this question, the student must perform the *Mayo* two-step analysis.

First, does the process involve an abstract concept? Yes. The facts indicate that the idea that using warm air to heat a furnace is better than using cold air is a fundamental principle.

Second, the student must determine whether the process claim contains an inventive concept sufficient to transform the abstract concept into a patent-eligible application. Specifically, is the claim directed to the abstract idea of heating a furnace with warm air or to an inventive application of that idea.

To answer this question, the student should identify and analyze any additional features of the claimed process. Here, the additional features of the claim include an intermediate air receptacle that is heated by an external device to a high temperature. A pipe transfers the heated air into the furnace.

These additional features make the process patent-eligible. The invention does more than just instruct users to use the principle that hot air is better at increasing furnace temperatures. Instead, it demonstrates how the principle can be used in an inventive process. The claimed process includes a law of nature and additional features that define the useful application of that principle. Moreover, the claim does not prevent others from using the heated air principle.

■ PROBLEM 4.2 ■

Scott Electric ("Scott") owns a patent on a method for monitoring an electric power grid. The method comprises the steps of collecting data from sensors placed at strategic locations in the power grid, analyzing the data using a clustering algorithm, and displaying the results to a user. The clustering algorithm is a known algorithm used for data analysis and the method steps are carried out on conventional computing hardware.

Scott sues General Power ("General") for patent infringement, alleging that General infringes his patented method. In response, General files a motion for summary judgment, asserting that Scott's patent is invalid for being directed to an abstract idea.

Is Scott's method eligible for patenting under 35 U.S.C. § 101?

Analysis

35 U.S.C. § 101 states that an inventor may obtain a patent on any (1) process, (2) machine, (3) manufacture, or (4) composition of matter. An invention is not eligible for patenting if it is directed to (1) abstract ideas, laws of nature or natural phenomena, and (2) the patent claims do not add enough to transform the nature of the claim into a patent eligible invention. Here, the asserted patent is directed toward an invention that uses a known algorithm to monitor an electric power grid. Thus, students should apply the *Mayo* two-part framework to analyze this question.

The first step of the analysis is concerned with the focus of the claims as a whole. Here, the method comprises the steps of collecting data from sensors placed at strategic locations in the power grid, analyzing the data using a clustering algorithm, and displaying the results to a user. Data is intangible. Thus, simply collecting data or information by itself is an abstract idea. Similarly, analyzing data using mental steps or an algorithm without more is also an abstract idea. Finally, displaying the results of an abstract process is also abstract. Thus, it is clear that Scott's claimed process is directed to an abstract idea.

The second step of the analysis concerns whether the claim elements add an inventive concept in the application of an abstract idea, law of nature or natural phenomena. Here, the claims operate in a power grid which is a tangible environment. However, limiting the abstract process of data collection, analysis and display to a power grid does not add enough to transform these mental steps into a patent eligible invention. Further, there is no evidence that the claims require anything more than conventional computer hardware to execute the method steps. Thus, under step two of the *Mayo* patent eligibility framework there is nothing present in the claims that would transform them into claims directed to patent eligible inventions. Accordingly, Scott's method for monitoring a power grid is ineligible for patenting under 35 U.S.C. § 101.

POINTS TO REMEMBER

- The patent claims define the invention. Accordingly, the focus of any patent analysis is on the language used in the claims to describe the invention.

- Processes, machines, compositions of matter, and manufactures are patent-eligible subject matter.

- Abstract concepts such as laws of nature, natural phenomena and abstract ideas are generally patent-ineligible.

- A claim involving an abstract concept may be patent-eligible if the abstract concept is only part of a larger invention that has an inventive concept.

- Whether an invention qualifies as patentable subject matter is only one of five general requirements an invention must meet to obtain patent protection. The remaining requirements are utility, novelty, nonobviousness, and enablement, each of which will be discussed in subsequent chapters.

CHAPTER 5

Utility, Disclosure, Novelty, and Nonobviousness

his chapter will summarize the novelty, utility, disclosure, and nonobviousness requirements for patentability. To obtain a patent, the law requires that an invention be new, useful, and a nonobvious improvement over the prior art. The law also requires that an applicant sufficiently disclose their invention in their patent application.

Most IP survey courses will devote significant time to the novelty and nonobviousness requirements. Congress revised the novelty statute in the America Invents Act ("AIA"), which was signed into law in 2011. However, the old law still applies to patents filed before March 16, 2013. Accordingly, students must understand the novelty requirement prior to the America Invents Act and how the law changed as it applies to patents filed after the AIA took effect.

Nonobviousness can be a complex legal analysis. As a starting point, students must analyze how a subject invention differs from existing prior art. Students must then consider a person of ordinary skill in the art ("PHOSITA") and whether this person would have been capable of arriving at the invention.

This chapter outlines the novelty, utility, disclosure, and nonobviousness requirements in a way that will allow you to systematically identify the issues and apply the correct legal rules to most exam questions.

UTILITY, DISCLOSURE, NOVELTY, AND NONOBVIOUSNESS REVIEW

Utility

35 U.S.C. § 101 states in part that "[w]hoever invents or discovers any new and useful process. . ." may obtain a patent. The utility requirement for patentability is derived from the word "useful." Generally, the utility requirement is easy to satisfy. The only categories where utility may be an issue include unsuccessful

inventions, some chemical and biotechnology inventions and inventions with questionable social benefits.

To satisfy the utility requirement, an invention must be credible, specific and substantial. An invention is credible if a person of ordinary skill in the art would accept that the invention is currently available for its purported use. A perpetual motion machine is an example of a device that lacks credible utility because scientific principles dictate that no such machine can exist.

An invention that has a real-world use, no matter how trivial, satisfies the specific and substantial requirement. For example, in *Juicy Whip, Inc. V. Orange Bang, Inc.*, the U.S. Court of Appeals for the Federal Circuit was asked to determine whether a patent covering a juice dispensing device satisfied the utility requirement. The patent disclosed a device with a glass bowl that contained an undrinkable liquid that was made to look like the liquid dispensed to a customer. The Federal Circuit found that the fact that the device altered one product to make it look like another satisfied the utility requirement under 35 U.S.C. § 101.[1]

The Disclosure Requirement

The disclosure requirement is set forth in 35 U.S.C. § 112(a). This section requires that a patent specification contain a written description of the invention that will enable a person of ordinary skill in the art to make or use the invention. In addition, § 112(a) requires that the patent specification "set forth the best mode contemplated by the inventor of carrying out his invention."[2] The following subsections will summarize the three elements of the disclosure requirement.

Enablement

The enablement requirement specifies that a patentee must sufficiently disclose their invention in the patent's specification such that it will enable one of ordinary skill in the art to make or use the invention without undue experimentation.[3] However, a patentee is not required to disclose well-known concepts. Instead, in *In re Wands*, the Federal Circuit listed a number of factors a court may consider in determining whether a specification has met the enablement requirement. These factors are known as the *Wands* factors and include: (1) the quantity of experimentation necessary, (2) the

---

[1] Juicy Whip, Inc. v. Orange Bang, Inc., 185 F.3d 1364, 1367 (Fed. Cir. 1999) ("The fact that one product can be altered to make it look like another is in itself a specific benefit sufficient to satisfy the statutory requirement of utility.")

[2] 35 U.S.C. § 112 (a).

[3] In re Wands, 858 F.2d 731, 737 (Fed. Cir. 1988).

amount of direction or guidance presented, (3) the presence or absence of working examples, (4) the nature of the invention, (5) the state of the prior art at the time of filing, (6) the relative skill of those in the art, (7) the predictability or unpredictability of the art, and (8) the breadth of the claims.[4]

Written Description

The written description requirement ensures that the inventor is in "possession" of what is claimed. The law requires the invention that is claimed be described in the specification of the patent application. Claims directed to an invention that is not disclosed in the patent specification are invalid for lack of written description.

For example, in *Gentry Gallery v. Berlin Corp.*, a defendant in a patent infringement suit claimed that the asserted patent to a sectional sofa was invalid due to lack of written description.[5] Specifically, the defendants argued that the specification described controls for the sectional sofa only being mounted on the top or side of the sofa's console.[6] In contrast, the asserted claims did not limit the position of the controls to the sofa console.[7] The Federal Circuit agreed that the claim failed the written description requirement because it claimed an invention that was not disclosed in the original patent.[8]

Best Mode

The best mode requirement warrants that the specification disclose the best way to make and use the invention. However, as of September 16, 2011, the failure of a patentee to disclose the best mode in her patent application cannot be a basis for attacking the patent on the grounds of invalidity or unenforceability.[9] As a result, a court cannot cancel or find a patent invalid or unenforceable for failing to disclose the best mode of the invention.

Novelty

An invention must be novel to be patented. The novelty requirement concerns two related issues. First, the invention must be new. Second, a patent applicant must file their patent application on their new invention in a timely manner.

---

[4] Id.

[5] Gentry Gallery, Inc. v. Berkline Corp., 134 F.3d 1473, 1478 (Fed. Cir. 1998).

[6] Id.

[7] Id.

[8] Id. at 1479.

[9] 35 U.S.C. § 282(b)(3)(A) (2017).

Recent changes in U.S. law have complicated the novelty requirement. The America Invents Act, signed into law in 2011, changed U.S. law with respect to novelty for all patent applications that were filed on or after March 16, 2013. The pre-AIA law still applies to applications filed before March 16, 2013. Thus, there are now two legal regimes for determining novelty.

Students should be familiar with both the pre and post AIA novelty provisions. In sum, the law changed the point in time at which novelty is measured. Pre-AIA law determines novelty based on the date of invention. In contrast, the law under the AIA determines novelty based on the filing date of the application. The following sections will summarize the pre-AIA law regarding the novelty requirement. The end of this section will include a summary of the law regarding post-AIA novelty.

Pre-AIA Novelty—§ 102(a)

A person is not entitled to a patent unless his invention is novel. To determine whether an invention is "novel" it must be compared to the prior art. "Prior art" is a term of art in patent law. Prior art is subject matter that existed before the date of invention of a patent. Possible prior art may include a printed publication or patent, anything known or used in a publicly accessible form, and anything on sale.

There are four events that may call the novelty of a patent into question if they occur or are performed by someone other than the inventor before the date of invention. Under 35 U.S.C. § 102(a), a person is entitled to a patent unless the invention was (1) known or (2) used by others in this country, or (3) patented or (4) described in a printed publication in this or a foreign country, before the invention thereof by the applicant for the patent. The "known" and "used" requirements refer to public knowledge and public use, and must be shown by clear and convincing evidence.[10] Public use is a non-secret use of the invention.[11] An invention is "patented" as of the date the patent is granted. Finally, a printed publication may include a number of things including a website, articles, white papers, books, conference papers, published patent applications, theses, etc. Whether a reference is a printed publication under the statute requires a determination of whether it is publicly accessible.[12]

---

[10] *See* Rosaire v. National Lead Co., 218 F.2d 72 (5th Cir. 1955), *cert. denied*, 349 U.S. 916 (1955) (Work that is done openly and in the ordinary course of business may be public use).

[11] *See id.*

[12] *See* In re Hall, 781 F.2d 897 (Fed. Cir. 1986);

Generally, a reference becomes public when it is available to at least one member of the public.[13]

If one or more of the requirements of § 102(a) is satisfied, the invention in question is said to be "anticipated" by the prior art. If a prior art reference "anticipates" an invention, that reference discloses, expressly or inherently, each and every element or step of the invention as defined in a patent claim.[14] In contrast, if even one element or step included in a patent claim is not disclosed in a single prior art reference, then that prior art reference does not anticipate the subject claim.

Determining whether an invention is novel under § 102(a) consists of three basic steps. First, the student must determine the date of invention. This date is the earlier of (1) when the inventor conceived of the invention or (2) the date the patent application is filed with the USPTO. Second, the student must identify any possible prior art. Third, the student compares each prior art reference to the patent claim at issue. If a single prior art reference discloses each and every element of the patent claim, that reference anticipates the claimed invention and renders it unpatentable. The timeline below is a visual illustration of how § 102(a) affects patentability and illustrates the steps in the analysis.

Novelty under Pre-AIA § 102(a)

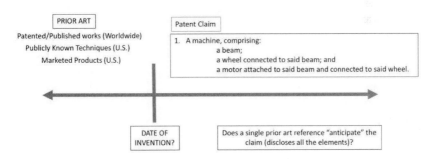

Pre-AIA Bars to Patentability—§ 102(b)

A person is not entitled to a patent unless her patent application was filed in a timely manner. 35 U.S.C. § 102(b) specifies that a person shall be entitled to a patent unless the invention was (1)

---

[13] See id.

[14] *See* Schering Corp. v. Geneva Pharmaceuticals, 339 F.3d 1373 (Fed. Cir. 2003).

patented or (2) described in a printed publication in this or a foreign country or (3) in public use or (4) on sale in this country, more than one year prior to the date of the application for patent in the U.S. In sum, 35 U.S.C. § 102(b) bars patentability if any of the four disclosure events occurs one year before the patent application is filed.

The first three statutory bar events are similar to their 102(a) counterparts in scope. However, note that "public use" can include the inventor's use of the invention as well as use by others. Concerning the on sale provision, § 102(b) also bars patentability of an invention if it is "ready for patenting" and subject to an offer for sale in the U.S. more than one year before the patent filing date.[15]

Timing is key to understanding how § 102(b) works. For example, in *In re Hall*, a dissertation disclosing the invention at issue was published more than one year before a patent application was filed disclosing the same invention.[16] The patent examiner rejected the patent under 35 U.S.C. § 102(b) in view of the dissertation. Finding that the dissertation was a publicly available printed publication, the Federal Circuit upheld a Board of Appeals decision, sustaining the patent examiner's rejection.[17] Similarly, in *Egbert v. Lippmann*, the court found that the inventor of corset steels had made public use of them for approximately eleven years before filing a patent application and therefore was barred from obtaining a patent.[18]

Determining whether an invention is novel under 35 U.S.C. § 102(b) consists of four basic steps. First, the student must identify the filing date of the patent. Second, the student must use the filing date to calculate the one year grace period. Third, the student must identify any possible prior art or novelty defeating events as set forth in the statute. Finally, the student compares each prior art reference or subject matter involved in the novelty defeating event to the patent claim at issue. If a single prior art reference or event that pre-dates the one-year grace period discloses each and every element of a patent claim, the claimed invention is unpatentable under § 102(b). The timeline below is a visual illustration of how the statutory bars under § 102(b) affect patentability and illustrates the steps in the analysis.

---

[15] Pfaff v. Wells Electronics, Inc., 525 U.S. 55, 67 (1998).

[16] *See* In re Hall, 781 F.2d 897, 898 (Fed. Cir. 1986).

[17] Id. at 900.

[18] *See* Egbert v. Lippmann, 104 U.S. 333 (1881).

Pre-AIA § 102 (b),(c),(d) Analysis

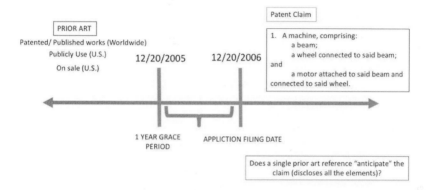

Finally, a doctrinal exception to § 102(b) is known as the experimental use exception. This exception states that the use of an invention in public by the inventor or another person, by way of experiment, to perfect the invention is not a public use. The doctrinal exception recognizes that in some cases an inventor must test their concept before they arrive at their final invention. For example, in *City of Elizabeth v. American Nicholson Pavement Co.,* the court decided that the experimental use exception applied to an inventor's public tests six years before his patent was filed on wooden pavement because the invention could not be feasibly tested in private, it remained under the inventor's control, and the inventor used the experiments in good faith to reduce his invention to practice.[19]

Other Pre-AIA Novelty Provisions

Most IP survey courses will focus on §§ 102(a) and 102(b). However, the pre-AIA novelty statute is a complex statute with several other provisions. This section will briefly summarize other circumstances that may prevent patentability under the novelty statute. These provisions apply to patent applications filed before March 16, 2013.

Abandonment—§ 102(c)

A person may not obtain a patent if he has abandoned the invention. There must be evidence of intent to abandon either

---

[19] City of Elizabeth v. American Nicholson Pavement Co., 97 U.S. 126, 136 (1877).

expressly or implicitly. Abandonment may be implied based on how long it took the inventor to file for a patent application.

Foreign Patenting—§ 102(d)

Under this provision an inventor cannot obtain a patent on an invention in the U.S. if (1) she filed for a patent in a foreign country and that patent issued before she filed in the U.S., or if (2) she filed for a patent in a foreign country and failed to apply for a patent in the U.S. within 12 months of the foreign filing.

Secret Prior Art—§ 102(e)

35 U.S.C. § 102(e) addresses how to deal with the peculiar timing of the patent prosecution process. The patent office publishes filed patent applications eighteen months after they are filed. This provision establishes that subject matter disclosed in a U.S. patent application or patent is prior art as of its filing date even if the application or patent has yet to be published by the patent office.

Derivation—§ 102(f)

A person is not entitled to obtain a patent on an invention that he did not invent. A successful challenge under this provision establishes that the invention was conceived by another inventor before the applicant and that the complete invention was conveyed to the applicant. Generally, these issues are determined in lengthy derivation proceedings at the USPTO.

Priority—§ 102(g)

Patent rights are established in the inventor who has priority in the invention. Under 35 U.S.C. § 102(g), the inventor who reduced the invention to practice without abandoning it has priority in the invention unless another inventor first conceived of the invention and diligently reduced it to practice without abandoning, suppressing or concealing the invention. The key to understanding how the priority provision works is to understand the terms conception, reduction to practice and reasonable diligence.

Conception is the formation in the mind of the inventor of a definite idea of a complete and operative invention.[20] An inventor has achieved conception when she knows how to make a working invention.

There are two ways an invention can be reduced to practice—actual and constructive. An inventor actually reduces an invention to

---

[20] 3A-10 Chisum on Patents § 10.04 (2017). ("Conception is the mental formulation and disclosure by the inventor of a complete idea for a product or process.").

practice when she "(1) constructs a product or performs a process that is within the scope of the patent claims, and (2) demonstrates the capacity of the inventive idea to achieve its intended purpose."[21] In contrast, when an applicant files an enabling patent application on an invention, that invention has been constructively reduced to practice.[22]

The statute requires the first inventor to conceive of the invention to exercise reasonable diligence in reducing the invention to practice. In practice, this means that if the inventor stopped working on the invention after conception, he must explain why his efforts were still reasonably diligent. Examples of valid reasons for why an inventor might stop working on an invention but still be reasonable diligent include, vacation, serious illness or some accident outside of the inventor's control that disrupts her work or work environment.[23] In contrast, courts have held that a long vacation or insufficient financial resources were not valid excuses for an inventor to discontinue their work on a project.[24]

Novelty After the America Invents Act

The America Invents Act was signed into law in 2011. The law is the most significant patent legislation to be enacted since the 1952 Patent Act.

Prior to the AIA, the U.S. was a "first to invent" country. The first person to invent the invention was given priority. In contrast, much of the rest of the world followed a "first to file" paradigm. This means that the first applicant to file an application for the invention was given priority. With the enactment of the AIA, the U.S. has adopted a hybrid system that many refer to as the "first inventor to file." This change took effect on March 16, 2013. Thus, the filing date of a patent application is central to understanding how the new novelty provisions under the AIA operate.

Under 35 U.S.C. § 102(a) as modified by the AIA, there are six categories of prior art if they occur before the effective filing date of the claimed invention: (1) patents, (2) printed publications, (3) public use, (4) on sale, (5) otherwise available to the public, and (6) the invention was described in a issued patent or published patent application.

Students should understand at least two changes from the pre-AIA novelty statute. First, prior art is now determined based solely

---

[21] Id. at § 10.06.

[22] Id. at § 10.05.

[23] Id.

[24] Id.

on the effective filing date of a patent application which deemphasizes the date of invention. Second, there is no longer a requirement that some novelty defeating events, e.g., public use or sale, occur in the U.S.

In the new version of 35 U.S.C. § 102(b), the AIA sets forth certain disclosures that will not be considered prior art under 102(a). First, if the disclosures were "made 1 year or less before the effective filing date of the claimed invention" any disclosure coming directly or indirectly from the inventor or joint inventor or made by others after a public disclosure by the inventor or joint inventor is not prior art. Second, a patent or patent application on the invention filed by another before the effective filing date of the claimed invention is not prior art if (1) the earlier filer derived the invention from the later filer, (2) the earlier filer filed after a public disclosure by the later filer or (3) the subject matter and claimed invention disclosed were owned by the same person or subject to an obligation of assignment to the same person no later than the effective filing date of the claimed invention.

Nonobviousness

35 U.S.C. § 103 states that a patent cannot be obtained for an invention that would have been obvious to a person having ordinary skill in the art before the invention date (Pre-AIA) or before the effective filing date (Post-AIA) of the invention. The nonobviousness requirement differs from the novelty requirement. Under novelty, an anticipatory prior art reference must disclose each and every element of the claimed invention. In contrast, a claim may be found obvious in view of prior art in combination with the knowledge and skill of a person of ordinary skill in the art and/or in combination with other prior art references.

Under 35 U.S.C. § 103, a claim is obvious "if the differences between the claimed invention and the prior art are such that the claimed invention as a whole would have been obvious before the effective filing date of the claimed invention to a person having ordinary skill in the art." Assessing whether a claimed invention is obvious includes several steps beginning with factual inquiries.[25] The following section summarizes the framework for determining nonobviousness.

Determine the Scope and Content of the Prior Art

The first step in the obviousness inquiry is to determine the scope and content of the prior art. The scope of the prior art falls into

---

[25] *See* Graham v. John Deere Co., 383 U.S. 1, 86 S. Ct. 684 (1966); KSR Int'l Co. v. Teleflex Inc., 550 U.S. 398, 127 S. Ct. 1727 (2007).

two categories. First, there are references in the same technical field as the claimed subject matter. Second, there is prior art in other fields that a person of ordinary skill might use to solve the problem the invention at issue purports to solve.[26]

Determine the Differences Between the Claims and the Prior Art

Next, students should determine the differences between the prior art identified in step one and the patent claims at issue. That is, what elements of the patent claims are not disclosed by the prior art. The obviousness inquiry will focus on those differences.

Determine the Level of Ordinary Skill in the Art

Third, students must ascertain the level of ordinary skill in the art. A person having ordinary skill in the art must have "the capability of understanding the scientific and engineering principles applicable to the pertinent art."[27] In order to determine the level of skill of a person having ordinary skill in the art, several factors may be considered, such as: (1) the educational level of the inventor; (2) type of problems encountered in the art; (3) prior art solutions to those problems; (4) rapidity with which innovations are made; (5) sophistication of the technology; and (6) educational level of active workers in the field.[28]

Determine if the Subject Matter Is Obvious

Given the first three determinations, students are now in a position to determine if the claimed subject matter would have been obvious to one of ordinary skill in the art. Consider the differences between the prior art and the patent claims and the level of ordinary skill in the art. Ask whether a person of ordinary skill in the art, given the prior art and faced with the problem the claimed subject matter addresses, "be led naturally to the solution adopted in the claimed invention or at least would naturally view that solution as an available alternative."[29] For example, if a person of ordinary skill in the art would view the claims at issue as a predictable variation to the prior art it, the claims are likely obvious and not patentable under § 103.[30] *KSR v. Teleflex* signaled a shift in focus from determining what the prior art discloses to also considering what a person having ordinary skill in the art can do. Accordingly, courts

---

[26] 2–5 Chisum on Patents § 5.03 (2017).

[27] Ex parte Hiyamizu, 10 U.S.P.Q.2d 1393 (P.T.O. Apr. 28, 1988).

[28] Daiichi Sankyo Co., LTD. V. Apotex, Inc., 501 F.3d 1254, 1256 (Fed. Cir. 2007).

[29] 2–5 Chisum on Patents § 5.04A (2017).

[30] KSR Int'l Co. v. Teleflex Inc., 550 U.S. 398, 417 (2007).

may take into account inferences and creative steps that a person having ordinary skill in the art would employ.

Note Secondary Considerations

Lastly, the students should analyze any secondary considerations that can overcome an obviousness determination. These secondary considerations include (1) commercial success; (2) industry praise and unexpected results; (3) copying by competitors; (4) industry skepticism the invention would work; (5) evidence of licensing; and (6) a long-felt, but unresolved need.[31] For example, the commercial success of the claimed invention may evidence nonobviousness by demonstrating the commercial demand for the solution. Evidence that the invention performed better in the industry than originally expected may also demonstrate nonobviousness. Finally, evidence that the claimed subject matter meets a long-felt need may support an argument that the claimed subject matter is nonobvious. In each case, the patentee must prove that a nexus exists between the secondary consideration and the merits of the claimed invention.

 UTILITY, DISCLOSURE, NOVELTY, AND NONOBVIOUSNESS CHECKLIST

With the above Review in mind, the Utility, Disclosure, Novelty, and Nonobviouness Checklist is presented below.

A. **UTILITY.** Determine whether the invention at issue meets the utility requirement. An invention that satisfies the utility requirement is credible, specific, and substantial.

  1. **Credible.** A credible invention is one that a person of ordinary skill in the art would believe exists and can perform its purported purpose.

  2. **Specific and Substantial.** A specific and substantial invention has real world use.

B. **DISCLOSURE.** Determine whether the patent specification describing the invention meets the disclosure requirements.

  1. **Enablement.** A patent specification meets the enablement requirement if it allows one of ordinary skill in the art to make or use the invention without undue experimentation.

---

[31] Transocean Offshore Deepwater Drilling, Inc. v. Maersk Drilling USA, Inc., 699 F.3d 1340, 1349 (Fed. Cir. 2012).

2. **Written Description.** A patent specification meets the written description requirement if it describes the invention that is being claimed in the patent. This requirement prevents potential patentees from acquiring rights in an invention they did not properly disclose.

3. **Best Mode.** A patent specification meets the best mode requirement if it discloses the best way to make and use the invention.

C. **NOVELTY.** Determine whether the invention is novel. Is the invention new? Was the patent application for the invention timely filed? Also, students should consider whether the pre-AIA or post-AIA requirements apply.

1. **Pre-AIA Novelty—§ 102(a).**

   a. **Determine the Date of Invention.** For the patent or patent application at issue, determine the date of invention. The date of invention is the earlier of the date the invention was conceived (if the inventor exercised diligence in reducing it to practice) or the date a patent application on the invention was filed.

   b. **Identify Possible Prior Art.** Prior art is subject matter that existed before the date of invention of a patent. Prior art can include patents, publications, anything known or used in a publicly accessible form, and anything on sale.

   c. **Novelty Defeating Events.** Under § 102(a), an invention is anticipated and therefore not novel if one of four events occur before its date of invention.

      1. **Known.** If the invention was publicly known before the given date of invention then it is not novel.

      2. **Used.** If the invention was used by others in the U.S. before the given date of invention then it is not novel.

      3. **Patented in This or a Foreign Country.** If the invention was patented in the U.S. or a foreign country before the given date of invention then it is not novel.

      4. **Described in a Printed Publication in This or a Foreign Country.** If the invention was described in a printed publication in the U.S. Or a

foreign country before the given date of invention then it is not novel.

d.   **Compare Each Prior Art Reference to the Claimed Invention.** Prior art is said to anticipate a claimed invention if it discloses expressly or inherently each and every element or step of the claim.

2.   **Pre-AIA Bars to Patentability—§ 102(b).**

a.   **Determine the Filing Date of the Patent.** When was the application for the patent filed?

b.   **Determine the beginning of the One Year Grace Period.** Count back one year from the filing date of the patent application. It is possible that anything that occurs before this date may defeat the novelty of the subject invention under § 102(b).

c.   **Novelty Defeating Events.** Under § 102(b), an invention is anticipated and therefore not novel if one of four events occur more than one year before the patent application on the invention was filed.

1.   **Patented in This or a Foreign Country.** If the invention was patented in the U.S. or a foreign country more than one year before the filing date of invention then it is not novel.

2.   **Described in a Printed Publication in This or a Foreign Country.** If the invention was described in a printed publication more than one year before the filing date of invention then it is not novel.

3.   **Public Use.** If the invention was used in public in the U.S. more than one year before the filing date of invention then it is not novel. Note that the experimental use exception may apply if the inventor or another used the invention in public to perfect it.

4.   **On Sale.** If the invention was on sale in the U.S. more than one year before the filing date of invention then it is not novel.

d.   **Compare Each Prior Art Reference to the Claimed Invention.** Prior art is said to anticipate a claimed invention if it discloses expressly or inherently each and every element or step of the claim.

3. **Post-AIA Novelty.** The AIA novelty requirements apply to all patents filed on and after March 16, 2013.

    a. **Determine the Effective Filing Date of the Patent Application.** When was the application for patent filed? Prior art is determined based on the effective filing date.

    b. **Post-AIA § 102(a).** If they occur before the effective filing date of the claimed invention, the following conduct or documents may be considered prior art: (1) patents, (2) printed publications, (3) public use, (4) on sale, (5) otherwise available to the public, and (6) the invention was described in an issued patent or published patent application. Note that the statute no longer requires the invention be used or on sale in the U.S.

    c. **Post-AIA § 102(b).** Certain disclosures are no longer considered prior art under § 102(b).

        1. **Disclosures Made One Year or Less Before the Effective Filing Date.** Any disclosure made one year or less before the effective filing date directly or indirectly by the inventor or joint inventor or made by others after a public disclosure by the inventor or joint inventor is not prior art.

        2. **Disclosures in Applications and Patents.** A patent or patent application on the invention filed by another before the effective filing date of the claimed invention is not prior art if (1) the earlier filer derived the invention from the later filer, (2) the earlier filer filed after a public disclosure by the later filer or (3) the subject matter and claimed invention disclosed were owned by the same person or subject to an obligation of assignment to the same person no later than the effective filing date of the claimed invention.

4. **NONOBVIOUSNESS.** Determine whether the invention is nonobvious.

    a. **Determine the Scope and Content of the Prior Art.** How would you characterize the invention? What problem does the invention solve? Identify relevant prior art in the same technical field as the patent claim at issue or that solves a similar problem.

b. **Determine the Difference Between the Claimed Invention and the Prior Art.** What elements of the patent claim at issue is not disclosed by the prior art?

c. **Ascertain the Level of Ordinary Skill in the Art.** What is the technological area of invention? A person having ordinary skill in the art must have the requisite skills, education or experience to understand the principles applicable to the pertinent art. Also, remember that a person of ordinary skill is presumed to know all the relevant prior art.

d. **Determine if the Subject Matter Is Obvious?** Against the background of the first three steps, determine whether subject matter is obvious or nonobvious. Is the subject matter a predictable variation that a person having ordinary skill in the art could implement? Would a person having ordinary skill in the art develop the subject matter from a technique known to improve other devices? Take into account inferences and creative steps that a person having ordinary skill in the art would employ.

e. **Make Note of Secondary Considerations.** Secondary considerations may serve as evidence that the invention in question is not obvious. These secondary considerations include: (1) commercial success; (2) industry praise and unexpected results; (3) copying by competitors; (4) industry skepticism the invention would work; (5) evidence of licensing; and (6) a long-felt, but unresolved need.

ILLUSTRATIVE PROBLEMS

Here are two problems that illustrate how the Checklist can be used to resolve patent utility, disclosure, novelty, and nonobviousness questions.

■ PROBLEM 5.1 ■

Café, Inc. ("Café"), a California corporation, develops coffee accessories such as cups, coffee makers, and mugs. In 2008, Walmart contacted Café because it was interested in purchasing coffee lids to sell in its U.S. stores. In response, Café sent Walmart a fax describing a new spill-proof coffee cup lid. Café had recently completed development and testing on the new spill-proof coffee cup lid. Café offered Walmart a price of $0.05 per lid for an order of 100,000 lids to be delivered within two months of the order being placed. The fax indicated that payment was due 60 days after delivery. Walmart never responded to the fax or made a counter offer, and Café did not sell its lids to Walmart or any other entity until 2016.

Café filed a patent on its coffee lid on April 2, 2010. In 2017, Café sued Wonder Labs ("Wonder") for infringing several claims of its patent directed to a spill-proof coffee cup lid. In response, Wonder contends that Café's patent is invalid under 35 U.S.C. § 102(b). Café contends that it did not sell its lids in 2008 and it would have never sold its lids to Walmart because Walmart's counter offer would likely have been unfavorable.

Discuss.

Analysis

Problem 5.1 asks you to determine whether Café has a valid patent on the spill-proof coffee lid. Specifically, whether Café's patent is barred under 35 U.S.C. § 102(b). Because the patent was filed in 2010, it will be analyzed under the pre-AIA § 102(b).

Under 35 U.S.C. § 102(b), a patent is barred if the invention was (1) patented or (2) described in a printed publication in this or a foreign country or (3) in public use or (4) on sale in this country, more than one year prior to the date of the application for patent in the U.S. Here, it is clear that the event in question, Café's fax to Walmart, occurred more than one year before Café filed a patent application on the cup lid. Thus, the issue is whether Café's fax was an offer to sell the invention.

Section 102(b) bars patentability of an invention if it is "ready for patenting" and subject to an offer for sale in the U.S. more than one year before the patent filing date. First, there is a strong argument that the cup lids were "ready for patenting." The facts indicate that Café had completed development and testing of the lids in 2008. Second, the facts seem to indicate that Café made an offer to sell its cup lids to Walmart. The fax contained price, delivery and payment terms, all of which are elements of a commercial offer to sell goods. Finally, Café's contention that it would not have gone through with the sale should be given little weight in the presence of documentary evidence of an offer to sell. Thus, it is likely that Café's patent is barred under § 102(b) and therefore invalid.

■ PROBLEM 5.2 ■

Claim 1 of Allied Engineering's ("Allied") patent application is directed to "tools used for demolition that can be attached to a single detachable arm, wherein the single detachable arm can be attached to a mobile platform such as a tractor, bulldozer, crane, or dump truck." Allied contends that their invention is a major innovation in the construction equipment field.

During examination, the patent examiner discovers two prior art references, both patents. The first reference, "Scavenger" discloses a system of detachable jaws for an excavator arm. The Scavenger system allows the jaws of the excavator arm to be changed easily as a unit. The second reference, "Hook" discloses a front-end loader for moving dirt with a detachable arm attached to a front bucket. The detachable arm can be replaced by other arms having different curvatures that allow the loader to vary the angle at which the front bucket operates. Hook extols the benefits of having multiple arm configurations to perform various loading jobs.

The examiner determines that a person having ordinary skill in the art, having knowledge of Scavenger and Hook, would arrive at Allied's claimed invention. Thus, in view of Scavenger and Hook, the examiner rejects claim 1 as obvious.

In response, Allied argues that a person of ordinary skill in the art would not combine the Scavenger and Hook references because it would result in a front-end loader with excavator jaws. Such a device would be of no use in the construction field. Further, Allied argues that a person of ordinary skill in the art would not use Hook to solve the problem their invention purports to solve because Hook emphasizes the benefits of having many detachable arms. Allied does not challenge the examiner's finding characterizing the skill and experience of a person of ordinary skill in the construction equipment field.

Will Allied succeed in convincing the examiner that its patent claim is not obvious?

Analysis

Problem 5.2 is concerned with the test for nonobviousness under 35 U.S.C. § 103. Under § 103, a claim is obvious "if the differences between the claimed invention and the prior art are such that the claimed invention as a whole would have been obvious before the effective filing date of the claimed invention to a person having ordinary skill in the art." The determination whether the claim at issue is obvious is made in consideration of the scope and content of the prior art, the differences between the claim and the prior art, and the level of ordinary skill in the art.

Here, Allied's claim relates to machinery used in construction. Similarly, the prior art patents fall within the field of construction machinery. In addition, both Allied's claim and the prior art references concern problems that can be solved by the interchangeability of machine components. Thus, there is a strong argument that a person of ordinary skill in the art might refer to both the Scavenger and Hook references.

Second, students must assess the differences between the claimed invention and the prior art. Allied argues that one difference is that its claim discloses a detachable arm that can be attached to a mobile platform of various types. In contrast, Scavenger discloses detachable jaws for an excavator. Hook discloses detachable arms of different curvatures for a single front-end loader. Thus, neither reference seems to disclose a detachable arm that can connect to demolition tools and various mobile platforms.

Since Allied does not challenge the examiner's characterization of a person of ordinary skill in the art, the obviousness determination must be made considering the prior art and the differences between Allied's claim and the prior art. Allied first argues that a person of ordinary skill in the art would not combine the Scavenger and Hook references because the resulting combination would be useless. However, the literal combination of prior art references does not have to be operable to render claimed subject matter obvious. Instead, the question is whether the teaching of the prior art references can be combined. Here the references teach a detachable tool in the form of excavator jaws and a detachable arm that connects to a front-end loader. Since both the excavator and front-end loader are types of mobile platforms, there is a strong argument that a person of ordinary skill in the art would be motivated by the teaching of the detachable tool and arm to arrive at Allied's invention.

Allied also argues that the Hook reference endorses the use of multiple detachable arms and thus is the opposite of the single detachable arm approach of Allied's invention. A reference may not be used in an obviousness rejection if it discourages a person of ordinary skill in the art from taking the approach described in the patent claim at issue. Here, the Hook reference simply lists the benefits of a multiple detachable arm configuration. Listing the benefits is not the same as teaching away from a single detachable arm. Thus, there is a strong argument that the Hook reference would not discourage a person of ordinary skill in the art from using a single arm as is claimed in Allied's patent.

Finally, Allied could present evidence to the examiner of secondary factors to overcome a finding of nonobviousness. Allied claims its invention is a major innovation in the construction field. Secondary considerations that align with this claim could provide evidence that Allied's invention is nonobvious. Any concrete evidence of (1) commercial success, (2) industry praise and unexpected results, (3) copying by competitors, (4) industry skepticism the invention would work, (5) licensing, and (6) a long-felt, but unresolved need would help support Allied's argument.

In sum, absent evidence of nonobviousness based on secondary considerations, Allied will probably fail in arguing that its patent claim is not obvious. One having ordinary skill in the art could have been motivated to combine the teachings of Scavenger and Hook to arrive at Allied's claimed invention.

POINTS TO REMEMBER

- An invention must be credible, specific, and substantial to satisfy the utility requirement under 35 U.S.C. § 101. An invention is credible if a person of ordinary skill in the art would accept that the invention is currently available for its purported use. An invention that has a real world use, no matter how trivial, satisfies the specific and substantial requirement.

- A patentee must sufficiently disclose their invention in the patent's specification such that it will enable one of ordinary skill in the art to make or use the invention without undue experimentation. The written description requirement requires that the invention that is claimed be described in the specification of the patent application. The specification must also disclose the best way to make and use the invention.

- Under Pre-AIA 35 U.S.C. § 102(a), a person is entitled to a patent unless the invention was (1) known or (2) used by others in this country, or (3) patented or (4) described in a printed publication in this or a foreign country, before the invention thereof by the applicant for the patent.

- Pre-AIA 35 U.S.C. § 102(b) specifies that a person shall be entitled to a patent unless the invention was (1) patented or (2) described in a printed publication in this or a foreign country or (3) in public use or (4) on sale in this country, more than one year prior to the date of the application for patent in the U.S.

- The determination of whether a patent claim is obvious is made in consideration of the scope and content of the prior art, the differences between the claim and the prior art, and the level of ordinary skill in the art. The decision maker may consider evidence that can overcome an obviousness determination including (1) commercial success; (2) industry praise and unexpected results; (3) copying by competitors; (4) industry skepticism the invention would work; (5) evidence of licensing; and (6) a long-felt, but unresolved need.

CHAPTER 6

Patent Infringement

T his chapter will summarize the law concerning patent infringement. The statutory requirements for patentability discussed in Chapters four and five will provide students with a solid foundation for analyzing patent infringement issues. This chapter will discuss the basic steps in a patent infringement analysis. It will also review third-party liability under contributory and induced infringement. Finally, this chapter will review the most common defenses to patent infringement. An understanding of these concepts will allow a student to work through patent infringement questions that may arise on an IP survey exam.

PATENT INFRINGEMENT REVIEW

Patent infringement is a complex topic that is taught as a separate course in many law schools. In an IP survey course, coverage on this topic will vary greatly depending upon your instructor's familiarity and interest in patent law. At a minimum, students should understand how patent infringement is defined, the basic steps in a patent infringement lawsuit, the most common defenses to patent infringement, and what remedies might be available to a successful plaintiff in a patent lawsuit. This review begins with a summary of patent rights and then explains how those rights might be infringed.

Patent Rights

An owner of a U.S. patent has certain rights in her invention during the patent's term. She has the right to exclude others from making, using or selling the invention without her permission in the United States. She also has the right to prevent another from importing the invention into the U.S. Finally, she can transfer her rights in the patent to others in a variety of ways including by assignment or license. Patent infringement generally occurs when another exercises these rights without the patent owner's authorization during the patent's term.

Term

A patent's term begins on the date the patent issues. Generally, the patent term ends twenty (20) years from the patent's U.S. application date. At the end of its term, the patent expires and becomes part of the public domain—free for others to use and exploit.

Standing and Venue

A party may assert a claim for patent infringement if the infringement occurred during the patent's term. Generally, the patent owner has standing to sue for infringement. Assignees, partial assignees, and exclusive licensees of a patent may also have standing to sue.

Federal courts have exclusive jurisdiction to hear patent infringement cases. An alleged infringer may be sued in a jurisdiction where they reside or where the defendant has a regular and established business and has committed infringement. The Supreme Court recently held that a domestic corporation resides in its state of incorporation.[1]

Infringement

A person infringes a patent when they, without authority, make, use, offer to sell, or sell the patented invention within the U.S. or import the patented invention into the U.S. during the term of the patent. Patent infringement is defined in 35 U.S.C. § 271. Most IP survey courses will cover direct infringement (§ 271(a)), inducement (§ 271(b)), and contributory infringement (§ 271(c)). This section will begin with a discussion of claim construction and then summarize direct infringement.

Claim Construction

The outcome of a patent infringement lawsuit hinges on two determinations: (1) whether the patent claims at issue are valid[2] and (2) whether the patent claims at issue are infringed literally or under the doctrine of equivalents. The claims of a patent define the invention. Thus, in order to resolve an infringement dispute, the patent claims must be analyzed to determine the patent owner's legal rights. The process of determining a patent claim's scope and meaning is referred to as claim construction.

---

[1] TC Heartland LLC v. Kraft Foods Grp. Brands LLC, 137 S. Ct. 1514, 1521 (2017).

[2] Chapters 4 and 5 address patent validity issues.

Claim construction is a matter of law.[3] Claim construction is a complex process in which the court is asked to determine the meaning of both technical claim language and common terms. Generally, claim terms are given their ordinary and customary meaning.[4] Claim terms are construed at the time of the invention and from the perspective of a person having ordinary skill in the art.

The claims themselves provide substantial information about their meaning. However, courts may rely on additional evidence to interpret claim language. While there is no strict formula, in *Phillis v. AWH Corp.*, the Federal Circuit provided some guiding principles for claim construction. The opinion explained that a court may consider both extrinsic and intrinsic evidence to construe claims.

Intrinsic evidence is the primary basis for claim construction. Therefore, intrinsic evidence takes precedence and is given greater weight than extrinsic evidence. Examples of intrinsic evidence include the patent's specification, other claims in the patent, the patent's prosecution history, the cited prior art, other patents that are related to the patent at issue, and the claim's preamble. Generally, the specification is the best tool to determine the meaning of claim language. However, limitations from the specification should not be read into the claims.[5] For example, in *Burke, Inc. v. Bruno Indep. Living Aids, Inc.*, the court held that the claim term "floor pan" could not be limited to mean a sheet pan made out of sheet metal even though the patent specification described a floor pan composed of sheet metal in a single pane.[6]

So long as it does not contradict intrinsic evidence, extrinsic evidence can also be considered when construing the meaning of claims. Extrinsic evidence generally includes expert testimony, dictionary or treatise definitions, and inventor testimony. The court in *Phillis v. AWH Corp.* explained that extrinsic evidence is less reliable than intrinsic evidence because it includes information that was not generated as part of the patenting process. Accordingly, extrinsic evidence is best suited for when there is ambiguity in construing the meaning of a claim term that cannot be resolved by intrinsic evidence.

To determine whether a patent claim is infringed, the claim is compared to the accused product or process. The accused product or process is identified by the patent owner as the product or process

---

[3] *See e.g.,* Markman v. Westview Instruments, 52 F.3d 967 (Fed. Cir. 1995) (en banc).

[4] Phillis v. AWH Corporation, 415 F.3d 1303, 1312–13 (Fed. Cir. 2005) (en banc).

[5] *See e.g.,* Burke, Inc. v. Bruno Indep. Living Aids, Inc., 183 F.3d 1334 (Fed. Cir. 1999).

[6] *See id.* at 1340.

that infringes the claimed invention. To be successful in a claim for infringement, the patent owner must show that each and every element of the asserted patent claim or its substantial equivalent is present in the accused product or process.

Direct Infringement

A person that performs each step of a claimed method or sells or makes a product that includes each element of a claimed invention directly infringes that patent claim. Direct infringement can occur literally or under the doctrine of equivalents.

Literal Infringement

A patent claim is literally infringed if each and every element or step in the subject claim is present in the accused product or process. This analysis requires the claim language to be closely compared with the alleged infringing device. For example, in *Larami Corp. v. Amron*, the claimed invention was directed to a water gun. The asserted claim described the water gun as having a water tank located *inside* the water gun's housing. The defendant successfully argued that its water gun did not infringe the asserted claim because its water tank was located *outside* of the water gun's housing.[7] Thus, if one element of a claim is not present in the accused product then there is no literal infringement.

The Doctrine of Equivalents

If an asserted patent claim is not literally infringed, the accused product may still infringe under the doctrine of equivalents. The doctrine of equivalents is a judicial doctrine that acknowledges the impreciseness of using words to define an invention. In analyzing whether a claim is infringed under the doctrine of equivalents, the court still makes an element by element comparison of the claim to the accused product. If the difference between a claim element and the element of the accused product is insubstantial, that claim element is infringed under the doctrine of equivalents. However, to find an entire claim infringed, a plaintiff must show that each and every element of the asserted claim or its equivalent is presented in the accused product.

Indirect Infringement

A patent owner may also enforce a patent against indirect infringers. Indirect infringers may include a person that encourages another to infringe a patent or a component supplier that contributes

---

[7] Larami Corp. v. Amron, 27 U.S.P.Q.2D (BNA) 1280, 1281 (E.D. Pa. Mar. 11, 1993).

to the manufacture of an infringing product. The law characterizes infringing activities as inducement under § 271(b) or contributory infringement under § 271(c). The following subsections summarize the law for inducement and contributory infringement.

Induced Infringement

Inducement involves an inducer and a direct infringer. An inducer that causes another to directly infringe a patent is liable for induced infringement. To succeed in a cause of action for induced infringement, the patent owner must prove that (1) the induced conduct of the direct infringer is infringement of the patent[8] and (2) that the inducer had the requisite intent.[9] To show intent, the patent owner must prove that the inducer intended to cause infringement of the patent and had knowledge of the patent, or was willfully blind to the patent's existence.[10]

Contributory Infringement

An entity that sells or imports a component of a patented item or for use in a patented process may be liable for contributory infringement if the component constitutes a material part of the invention and is not a staple article of commerce.[11] For liability to attach, the law also requires that the contributory infringer have known that the component was especially made or adapted for use in infringing the asserted patent. Specifically, the contributory infringer must have known about the patent and by her actions, intended to infringe the patent.[12]

Defenses to Patent Infringement

This section summarizes defenses to patent infringement that are generally covered in an IP survey course.

Invalidity

An invalid patent claim cannot be infringed. Thus, it is common for a defendant in a patent infringement suit to argue that the asserted claims in a patent are invalid on one or more statutory grounds. These grounds are summarized in Chapters 4 and 5. For

---

[8] Charles Miller, *Some Views on the Law of Patent Infringement by Inducement*, 53 J. Pat. Off. Soc'y 86, 102 (1971) ("Liability under 35 U.S.C. 271(b) requires the existence of direct infringement by another party which is actionable under 35 U.S.C. 271(a)").

[9] Glob.-Tech Appliances, Inc. v. SEB S.A., 563 U.S. 754, 766 (2011).

[10] *Id.* at 769.

[11] 35 U.S.C. § 271(c).

[12] *See e.g.,* Aro Mfg. Co. v. Convertible Top Replacement Co., 377 U.S. 476, 525 (1964).

example, a patent claim may be held invalid and therefore unenforceable because it is not novel, is obvious, is not enabled or sufficiently described, or because it is directed to unpatentable subject matter. Invalidity is claim specific—a defendant must invalidate each asserted claim.[13]

Experimental Use

In defense to patent infringement, a defendant may assert the experimental use defense. The experimental use defense is narrow and rarely successful. However, students should still understand the basic framework of the defense.

The experimental use defense states that a person that makes or uses a patented invention to satisfy a curiosity, for their amusement, or for philosophical inquiry is not an infringer of the patent. However, an allegedly infringing act does not qualify for experimental use if it is in furtherance of the actor's legitimate business.[14] For example, in *Madey v. Duke*, the Federal Circuit found that Duke University's unauthorized use of patented lab equipment was not an experimental use because the use furthered the university's legitimate business objectives of conducting research.[15]

Inequitable Conduct

In defense to patent infringement, an alleged infringer may argue that the asserted patent was obtained improperly. This defense is referred to as inequitable conduct. All parties involved with prosecuting a patent application at the USPTO (e.g., the patent attorney, the inventor, etc.) owe a duty of candor to the patent office. Breach of the duty of candor may give rise to inequitable conduct.

The conduct in question must be material and the actor must have carried out the conduct with an intent to deceive the USPTO. Conduct is material if the patent examiner would not have issued the patent but for the misrepresentation or omission.[16] Examples of actions that are a breach of the duty of candor include failing to cite known prior art during prosecution of the patent or withholding information about events that might bar patentability of the invention. If an alleged infringer is successful at proving inequitable conduct, the entire patent is invalidated. A finding of inequitable conduct may also endanger other patents owned by the same patent owner and make additional remedies available to the defendant.

---

[13] See 35 U.S.C. § 288 (2017).

[14] Madey v. Duke Univ., 307 F. 3d 1351, 1362 (Fed. Cir. 2002).

[15] *See id.* at 1362–63.

[16] *See e.g.,* Therasense, Inc. v. Becton, Dickinson & Co., 649 F.3d 1276 (Fed. Cir. 2011).

Patent Exhaustion

The first unrestricted sale of a patented product exhausts the patentee's monopoly and control as to that product. The purchaser may not make new copies of the patented invention, but the purchased product can be resold and repaired by the purchaser without violating any patent rights. Thus, a purchaser can assert the defense of patent exhaustion to prevent a patent owner from asserting post sale control over the purchased product.[17]

Patent Misuse

Patent misuse occurs when a patent owner improperly attempts to exploit her patent. For example, patent misuse prohibits a patent owner from charging royalties on a licensee's sales where those sales did not result from use of the patent owner's patents.[18] Thus, the doctrine of patent misuse attempts to discourage a patent owner from using her patent in anticompetitive conduct by baring the patent owner from enforcing the patent against others.

Laches

An accused infringer may assert the defense of laches if the patent owner unreasonably delayed in filing a patent infringement suit. The defense is available if the accused infringer can show (1) the patentee's delay in filing suit was unreasonable and inexcusable and (2) the alleged infringer suffered injury or material prejudice that is attributable to the delay.[19] "A presumption of laches arises where a patentee delays bringing suit for more than six years after the date the patentee knew or should have known of the alleged infringer's activity."[20]

Remedies

Injunctive relief and damages are available remedies for patent infringement. This section summarizes these remedies.

Injunctions

There are two types of injunctive relief available to a plaintiff in a patent lawsuit—preliminary injunctions and permanent injunctions. In both instances, the court enjoins the defendant from making, using, selling or importing the claimed invention. However, both injunctions are separate equitable remedies with different legal

---

[17] Quanta Comput., Inc. v. LG Elecs., Inc., 553 U.S. 617, 638 (2008).

[18] *See e.g.,* Zenith Radio Corp. v. Hazeltine Research Inc., 339 U.S. 100 (1969).

[19] SCA Hygiene Prods. Aktiebolag v. First Quality Baby Prods., LLC, 807 F.3d 1311, 1317 (Fed. Cir. 2015).

[20] Id.

standards.[21] This subsection summarizes the requirements for obtaining both types of injunctions.

Preliminary Injunction

A court may grant a preliminary injunction before trial. The burden is on the plaintiff to present evidence that justifies the granting of a preliminary injunction. The court will consider four factors: (1) the plaintiff's reasonable likelihood of success on the merits, (2) whether the plaintiff will suffer irreparable harm in the preliminary injunction is not granted, (3) the balance of hardships is in the plaintiff's favor, and (4) the impact of the preliminary injunction on the public interest. Because there is limited information available to the court before trial, preliminary injunctions are generally difficult to obtain.

Permanent Injunction

After trial, a court may award a permanent injunction if the patent owner's patent is valid and infringed. In limited cases, a court will not award an injunction if it is not "essential to preserve the rights of the patentee and would cause the infringer irreparable damage."[22] Similar to preliminary injunctions, there is a four-factor test to determine whether the court should grant a permanent injunction. A plaintiff must show that (1) it has suffered irreparable injury, (2) remedies at law, such as monetary damages, are inadequate to compensate for that injury, (3) considering the balance of hardships between the plaintiff and the defendant, a remedy in equity is warranted, and (4) the public interest would not be disserved by a permanent injunction.[23]

Damages

A plaintiff may obtain monetary relief in the form of compensatory damages for patent infringement. Compensatory damages may be established using lost profits, an established royalty or a reasonable royalty.[24]

Established Royalty

First, a plaintiff may recover an amount based on an established royalty rate if the patent owner offers licenses to the patent at an

---

[21] Lerner Germany GmbH v. Lermer Corp., 94 F.3d 1575, 1577 (Fed. Cir. 1996).

[22] Milwaukee v. Activated Sludge, 69 F.2d 577, 593 (7th Cir. 1934).

[23] eBay Inc. v. MercExchange, L.L.C., 547 U.S. 388, 391 (2006).

[24] 7–20 Chisum on Patents § 20.01 (2017).

established royalty rate.[25] The established royalty rate is a uniform and freely negotiated rate "paid by a sufficient number of licensees."[26]

Lost Profits

Second, a plaintiff may also obtain lost profits if it is in competition with the defendant. To obtain lost profits a patent owner must prove that there was a reasonable probability that but for the infringer's sales "he would have made greater sales, charged higher prices or incurred lower expenses."[27] In order to satisfy this standard, a patent owner must present evidence of (1) demand for the product, (2) the absence of acceptable non-infringing substitutes, (3) that the plaintiff possessed the manufacturing and marketing capability to exploit the demand and (4) the amount of profit the patent owner would have made.[28]

Reasonable Royalty

Finally, if the patent owner cannot prove an established royalty or lost profits they may recover a reasonable royalty. A reasonable royalty is the least a plaintiff may obtain for the use of the made invention by the infringer.[29] A reasonable royalty is the amount that would have been agreed upon by willing parties if they had negotiated an agreement on the date the infringement began.[30] A comprehensive, but not exclusive, list of factors a court may consider in determining a reasonable royalty include:

"1.   The royalties received by the patentee for the licensing of the patent in suit, proving or tending to prove an established royalty.

2.   The rates paid by the licensee for the use of other patents comparable to the patent in suit.

3.   The nature and scope of the license, as exclusive or non-exclusive; or as restricted or non-restricted in terms of territory or with respect to whom the manufactured product may be sold.

4.   The licensor's established policy and marketing program to maintain his patent monopoly by not licensing

---

[25] 7–20 Chisum on Patents § 20.03 (2017).

[26] 7–20 Chisum on Patents § 20.06 (2017).

[27] 7–20 Chisum on Patents § 20.05 (2017).

[28] Panduit Corp. v. Stahlin Bros. Fibre Works, 575 F.2d 1152, 1156 (6th Cir. 1978).

[29] 35 U.S.C. § 284 (2017).

[30] Rite-Hite Corp. v. Kelley Co., Inc., 56 F.3d 1538, 1554 (Fed. Cir. 1995) (en banc), *cert. denied*, 516 U.S. 867 (1995).

others to use the invention or by granting licenses under special conditions designed to preserve that monopoly.

5.   The commercial relationship between the licensor and licensee, such as, whether they are competitors in the same territory in the same line of business; or whether they are inventor and promotor.

6.   The effect of selling the patented specialty in promoting sales of other products of the licensee; the existing value of the invention to the licensor as a generator of sales of his non-patented items; and the extent of such derivative or convoyed sales.

7.   The duration of the patent and the term of the license.

8.   The established profitability of the product made under the patent; its commercial success; and its current popularity.

9.   The utility and advantages of the patent property over the old modes or devices, if any, that had been used for working out similar results.

10.   The nature of the patented invention; the character of the commercial embodiment of it as owned and produced by the licensor; and the benefits to those who have used the invention.

11.   The extent to which the infringer has made use of the invention; and any evidence probative of the value of that use.

12.   The portion of the profit or of the selling price that may be customary in the particular business or in comparable businesses to allow for the use of the invention or analogous inventions.

13.   The portion of the realizable profit that should be credited to the invention as distinguished from non-patented elements, the manufacturing process, business risks, or significant features or improvements added by the infringer.

14.   The opinion testimony of qualified experts.

15.   The amount that a licensor (such as the patentee) and a licensee (such as the infringer) would have agreed upon (at the time the infringement began) if both had been reasonably and voluntarily trying to reach an agreement; that is, the amount which a prudent licensee—who desired, as a business proposition, to obtain a license to manufacture

and sell a particular article embodying the patented invention—would have been willing to pay as a royalty and yet be able to make a reasonable profit and which amount would have been acceptable by a prudent patentee who was willing to grant a license."[31]

Increased Damages and Attorney Fees

At its discretion, a court may triple the amount of damages awarded. Generally, the increase in damages is due to a showing of willful infringement or egregious conduct on behalf of the defendant. Proof of willful infringement requires a showing that the infringer acted despite an objectively high likelihood that its actions constituted infringement of a valid patent and that this risk was known or so obvious that the infringer should have known.[32]

A court may also award attorney fees to the prevailing party in exceptional cases.[33] An exceptional case "stands out from others with respect to the substantive strength of a party's litigating position (considering both the governing law and the facts of the case) or the unreasonable manner in which the case was litigated."[34] To determine whether a case is exceptional a court may consider various factors such as "frivolousness, motivation, objective unreasonableness (both in the factual and legal components of the case) and the need in particular circumstances to advance considerations of compensation and deterrence."[35]

 PATENT INFRINGEMENT CHECKLIST

With the above Review in mind, the Patent Infringement Checklist is presented below.

A. **PATENT RIGHTS.** Generally, patent infringement occurs when an entity exercises a patent owner's exclusive rights in an invention without their permission. The patent owner has the right to exclude others from making, using or selling the patented invention without their permission in the U.S.

---

[31] Ga.-Pacific Corp. v. United States Plywood Corp., 318 F. Supp. 1116, 1120 (S.D.N.Y. 1970).

[32] In re Seagate, 497 F.3d 1360, 1371 (Fed. Cir. 2007) (en banc).

[33] 35 U.S.C. § 285 (2017).

[34] Octane Fitness, LLC v. ICON Health & Fitness, Inc., 134 S. Ct. 1749, 1756 (2014).

[35] 7–20 Chisum on Patents § 20.03 [4][c][i] (2017).

1. **Patent Term.** Determine when the infringement occurred relative to the patent's term. The patent is free for others to exploit once it has expired.

2. **Standing.** Determine whether a party has standing to sue for infringement. Generally, the patent owner, assignees, partial assignees, and exclusive licensees have standing to sue.

B. **INFRINGEMENT.** A patent claim is infringed when each and every element of a patent claim or its equivalent is present in an accused device or process. Claim construction determines a claim's scope and meaning. To determine infringement, one compares the claim as construed to an accused device or process.

1. **Claim Construction.** Determine the ordinary and customary meaning of disputed claim terms at the time of the invention. Intrinsic evidence, such as the patent specification, other claims in the patent, the patent's prosecution history, the cited prior art, other patents that are related to the patent at issue, and the claim's preamble, is the primary basis for claim construction. Extrinsic evidence, such as expert testimony and the dictionary, may also be considered for claim construction so long as they do not contradict any intrinsic evidence.

2. **Direct Infringement.** A direct infringer is a person or entity that makes, uses, sells, or imports a product that includes each and every element of a claimed product or performs each and every step of a claimed method.

   a. **Literal Infringement.** A patent claim is literally infringed if each and every element or step in the subject claim is present in the accused product or process.

   b. **The Doctrine of Equivalents.** If the claim is not literally infringed, determine whether it is infringed under the doctrine of equivalents. In an element by element comparison of the claim, if the difference between the claim element and the element of the accused product is insubstantial, then the claim element is infringed under the doctrine of equivalents.

C. **INDIRECT INFRINGEMENT.** A person or entity that encourages another to infringe a patent or supplies components that are used in an infringing product may be liable for induced or contributory infringement.

1. **Induced Infringement.** Determine whether a person or entity caused another to directly infringe a patent. The patent owner must prove that the alleged inducer intended to cause infringement of the patent and had knowledge of the patent or was willfully blind to the patent's existence.

2. **Contributory Infringement.** An entity that sells or imports a component of a patented item or for use in a patented process may be liable for contributory infringement if the component constitutes a material part of the invention and is not a staple article of commerce. To be liable, the alleged contributory infringer must have known of the patent and intended to infringe the patent.

D. **DEFENSES TO PATENT INFRINGEMENT.** Determine whether the alleged infringer has a defense to patent infringement. In addition to asserting that an accused process or product does not infringe the asserted patent, a defendant may have other defenses available.

1. **Invalidity.** Determine whether the asserted patent claim is invalid. A patent claim may be held invalid because it is not novel, is obvious, is not enabled or sufficiently described or because it is directed to unpatentable subject matter.

2. **Experimental Use.** Determine whether the alleged infringer made an experimental use of the patented invention. A person that makes or uses a patented invention to solely to satisfy a curiosity, for their amusement, or for philosophical inquiry is not an infringer of the patent.

3. **Inequitable Conduct.** Determine whether the patent was obtained improperly by material conduct that was intended to deceive the USPTO. Conduct is material if the patent examiner would not have issued the patent but for the misrepresentation or omission.

4. **Patent Exhaustion.** Is the patent owner attempting to assert control over a patented product after it has been lawfully sold? The first unrestricted sale of a patented product exhausts the patentee's monopoly and control as to that product.

5. **Patent Misuse.** Is the patent owner attempting to improperly exploit the patent? The defense of patent misuse prevents a patent owner from enforcing a patent in a way that is anticompetitive.

6. **Laches.** Did the patent owner delay in filing suit? The defense of laches may be available if (1) the patentee's delay in filing suit was unreasonable and inexcusable and (2) the alleged infringer suffered injury or material prejudice that is attributable to the delay.

E. **REMEDIES.** Injunctive relief and damages are available remedies for patent infringement.

1. **Injunctions.** A court may grant a preliminary injunction before trial or a permanent injunction if the asserted patent is valid and infringed.

    a. **Preliminary Injunctions.** To determine whether a preliminary injunction is appropriate, a court will consider (1) the plaintiff's reasonable likelihood of success on the merits, (2) whether the plaintiff will suffer irreparable harm if the preliminary injunction is not granted, (3) the balance of hardships is in the plaintiff's favor, and (4) the impact of the preliminary injunction on the public interest.

    b. **Permanent Injunctions.** To obtain a permanent injunction a plaintiff must show (1) it has suffered irreparable injury, (2) remedies at law, such as monetary damages, are inadequate to compensate for that injury, (3) considering the balance of hardships between the plaintiff and the defendant, a remedy in equity is warranted, and (4) the public interest would not be disserved by a permanent injunction.

2. **Damages.** A plaintiff may obtain damages based on lost profits, an established royalty or a reasonable royalty.

    a. **Lost Profits.** If the patent owner is in competition with the defendant, they may obtain damages based on their lost profits. A patent owner must present evidence of (1) demand for the product, (2) the absence of acceptable non-infringing substitutes, (3) that the plaintiff possessed the manufacturing and marketing capability to exploit the demand and (4) the amount of profit the patent owner would have made.

    b. **Established Royalty.** If the patent owner offers licenses to the patent at an established royalty rate, then he may recover damages in an amount based on that established royalty rate.

    c. **Reasonable Royalty.** At a minimum, a patent owner may recover damages based on a reasonable royalty. A reasonable royalty is the amount that would have been agreed upon by willing parties if they had negotiated an agreement on the date the infringement began. A list of the *Georgia-Pacific* factors that may be considered to determine a reasonable royalty is included in Chapter 6 for your reference.

3. **Increased Damages and Attorney Fees.** A court may triple the amount of damages awarded if the infringement is willful or the defendant's conduct was egregious. In addition, a court may award attorney fees to the prevailing party in exceptional cases.

ILLUSTRATIVE PROBLEMS

Here are two problems that illustrate how the Checklist can be used to resolve patent infringement questions.

■ PROBLEM 6.1 ■

Alpha Corp. ("Alpha") manufactures and sells coffee makers in the United States. Mountain Coffee ("Mountain") is Alpha's main competitor. Mountain also manufactures and sells coffee makers in the U.S.

Alpha filed suit for patent infringement against Mountain, alleging that Mountain's single-serve beverage maker infringes claim 1 of Alpha's patent directed to a "Cartridge Brewing System." Claim 1 is reproduced below.

1. **A beverage brewer comprising:**

   a beverage cartridge having a beverage ingredient therein; and

   a brewer including a cartridge holder and an inlet needle,

   wherein when the beverage cartridge is positioned in the cartridge holder, the inlet needle pierces the beverage cartridge at a fixed position within the beverage brewer.

The parties dispute the meaning of the claim term *beverage ingredient*. The parties agree that *beverage ingredient* refers to a mixture that the beverage brewer uses to brew a single-serve drink. They also agree that *beverage ingredient* refers to tea or coffee. However, the parties dispute whether *beverage ingredient* has a more limited meaning in reference to ground coffee.

Alpha asserts that the term *beverage ingredient* means "an ingredient including tea or coffee to brew a beverage." In contrast, Mountain argues that the term *beverage ingredient* means "an ingredient for making a beverage including tea and coffee. When the beverage ingredient is coffee, the grind size must be between 0.20 mm–0.40 mm."

Alpha's patent specification uses the term *beverage ingredient* in several places throughout the patent. *Beverage ingredient* is used consistently to refer to ingredients contained in a beverage cartridge and used by the brewer to brew tea or coffee. There are several instances in which the specification describes the *beverage ingredient* without designating the grind size. In one portion of the patent, the specification details an experiment that found that coffee with a grind size between 0.20 mm and 0.40 mm produced coffee that was 10% stronger than the coffee used in Mountain's products. The patent also suggests that coffee grinds with a size between 0.20 mm and 0.40 mm be used in its beverage brewer to brew stronger coffee. Except for this portion of the specification, Alpha's patent refrains from mentioning any coffee grind size limitations when discussing the *beverage ingredient* throughout the remainder of the abstract, specification, and claims.

In support of its claim construction, Mountain points to the above-referenced discussion in Alpha's patent about coffee grind size. In addition, Mountain relies on testimony from its coffee brewing expert, Professor Moluslk. Professor Moluslk testified that one of ordinary skill in the art of coffee brewing would understand that Alpha's patent requires the use of coffee with a grind size between 0.20 mm and 0.40 mm.

How should the district court construe the claim term *beverage ingredient*?

Analysis

Problem 6.1 simulates a claim construction issue that may arise during a patent lawsuit. Students should discuss the law of claim construction and then apply the law to the facts to suggest how a district court might interpret the meaning of the term *beverage ingredient* during a Markman hearing.

Claim construction is a question of law. In determining the meaning of disputed claim terms, the court seeks to construe claim terms as would be understood by a person of ordinary skill in the art as of the effective filing date of the invention. The court may examine intrinsic evidence such as the words of the claims, the patent specification, the prosecution history, and extrinsic evidence to determine the meaning of disputed claim terms. Intrinsic evidence is given greater weight than extrinsic evidence.

The court should begin the claim construction process by focusing on the language of the claims themselves. Claims should be given their ordinary and customary meaning.

The specification describes the invention and sets the outer scope for the claims. Claims cannot be construed broader than the invention described in the specification. However, courts must also be careful not to read limitations from the specification into the claims.

Finally, if helpful, the court may consider extrinsic evidence such as expert testimony. Expert testimony can educate the court about the patented technology and how a person of ordinary skill in the art would understand the meaning of disputed claim terms. However, extrinsic evidence is viewed as less reliable than intrinsic evidence. Thus, the court cannot use extrinsic evidence to contradict the unambiguous meaning of a claim term as supported by intrinsic evidence.

Here, the parties dispute whether the claim term requires that when the beverage ingredient is coffee, the grind size must be between 0.20 mm–0.40 mm. For the following reasons, the court should construe the term *beverage ingredient* to mean "an ingredient including tea or coffee to brew a beverage" as proposed by the patentee, Alpha.

Beginning with the claim language itself, the plain and ordinary meaning of *beverage ingredient* is something included in the beverage cartridge that the beverage brewer will use to create a drinkable liquid—tea or coffee. The claim language does not restrict the grind size of the beverage ingredient.

The term *beverage ingredient* is used in the specification to refer to ingredients contained in a beverage cartridge. Further, the specification uses the term *beverage ingredient* in several instances without referencing grind size. While the specification does suggest the optimal grind size for coffee is 0.20 mm–0.40 mm, this does not require the court to construe the claims as narrowly as Mountain would like. The claim does not require a particular grind size for the *beverage ingredient*. Second, the court should not read limitations from the specification into the claims. Thus, a reading of the claims and specification indicate that the term *beverage ingredient* means "an ingredient including tea or coffee to brew a beverage."

Finally, Professor Moluslk's testimony does not warrant the court to adopt Mountain's proposed construction. The court must give the intrinsic evidence greater weight than extrinsic evidence such as expert testimony. Here, an analysis of the claims and the specification both lead to the conclusion that the meaning of the term *beverage ingredient* is clear and unambiguous. Professor Moluslk's testimony cannot be used by the court to contradict an unambiguous claim meaning.

In sum, for the reasons set forth above, the court should construe *beverage ingredient* as "an ingredient to brew a beverage" as proposed by Alpha.

■ PROBLEM 6.2 ■

Hazo makes the "Children's Play Mat" which is an inexpensive floor exercise mat made of soft material for developing children's physical, cognitive and social skills. It consists of several tiles with some of the tiles having various drawings on their surface. Some tiles have a drawing of one or two feet. Other tiles have drawings of one or two hands. The hands and feet are drawn in a "finger paint" style such that it looks like a child's foot or hand was dipped in paint and then placed on the tile. Additional tiles have block arrows that point in different directions.

Hazo obtains a patent in 2010 on the Children's Play Mat. The broadest claim reads:

1. An instructional floor exercise apparatus comprising:

    a plurality of tiles;

    wherein at least two of the plurality of tiles each comprise an anatomy indicium and a tile orientation indicium, wherein the orientation indicium indicates a direction; and

    wherein the anatomy indicium form a pattern that corresponds to a predetermined physical movement when the tiles are placed in a predetermined spatial relation to one another.

The image above shows a child playing on a Children's Play Mat. The patent was obtained over prior art, which disclosed a hard rubber mat with tiles that featured images of block arrows on them. Among the advantages of the Children's Play Mat over the prior art are its softer material and its inclusion of hands and feet that indicate physical movements that are simple for young children to understand.

In 2016, MatTech manufactured a children's playing surface that consists of hard rubber tiles that have interlocking edges, enabling them to be releasably attached to one another. The MatTech tiles have images of block arrows, hands and feet in a "finger paint" style similar, but not identical, to that of the Children's Play Mat. While they look normal in the light, the MatTech tiles also glow in the dark. Children play with MatTech's mat and Hazo's mat in a similar manner.

The MatTech product outsells the Hazo "Children's Play Mat" during the 2016 holiday shopping season. The CEO of Hazo is furious that its "ideas" were "stolen" by MatTech.

Discuss all relevant legal issues, claims, and arguments of both parties. Determine who is likely to prevail and why.

Analysis

This question gives students an opportunity to address two basic issues in patent litigation. First, does MatTech's competing product infringe claim 1 of Hazo's patent? Second, is the Children's Play Mat claim valid in view of the prior art?

Patent infringement analysis involves interpreting the claim language, assessing the accused product and then applying the claims to the accused product. For a patent claim to be literally infringed, every limitation in the claim must be set forth in the accused product.

Here, the accused product is the MatTech playing surface. Identify and compare the elements of Hazo's claim 1 to the MatTech product. The MatTech playing surface has a plurality of tiles. MatTech's tiles also have anatomy indicium (hands/feet) and tile orientation indicium that indicate a direction (block arrows). Finally, because children play with MatTech's mat in a way similar to Hazo's mat, the hands and feet tiles of MatTech's product likely form a pattern that correspond to predetermined physical movement as required in the claim. Thus, there seems to be a strong argument that the MatTech product infringes claim 1 of Hazo's patent.

Note that MatTech mat has several features that are not in Hazo's claim 1. For example, MatTech's mat is made of hard rubber, has interlocking tiles and glows in the dark. However, the presence of these additional features does not support an argument that the MatTech mat does not infringe Hazo's claim 1.

Finally, MatTech may assert that claim 1 of Hazo's patent is invalid in view of the prior art. Specifically, that claim 1 is obvious in view of the prior art. Here, the problem states that Hazo's patent was granted in view of prior art that disclosed a mat with block arrows. The key question is whether, at the time of the invention, it would have been obvious for a person having ordinary skill in the art to improve upon the prior art mat by adding tiles with painted hands and feet that indicate physical movements. The problem does not provide enough facts to resolve the issue, but students should at least mention that invalidity should be explored by MatTech as a possible defense to patent infringement.[36]

POINTS TO REMEMBER

- Direct infringement occurs when a person sells or makes a product that includes each and every element of a patent claim or performs each step of a method patent claim without the authorization of the patent owner.

- To determine infringement, compare the patent claim to an accused device or process. Claim terms are given their ordinary and customary meaning at the time of invention. Courts will rely primarily on intrinsic evidence to construe claim terms.

- Generally, a person that causes another to directly infringe a patent may be liable for induced infringement if the inducer had knowledge of the patent and intended to cause infringement.

- A successful inequitable conduct defense requires a showing that the accused party's conduct was material and done with an intent to deceive the USPTO.

- A successful patent owner in a patent infringement suit may obtain monetary relief in the form of damages. At minimum, the patent owner can recover a reasonable royalty. A reasonable royalty is an amount the parties would have negotiated on the date the infringement began.

---

[36] *See* problem 5.2 for a detailed discussion of how to address an obviousness essay question.

CHAPTER 7

Copyright Requirements and Copyrightable Subject Matter

his chapter reviews the law concerning copyright requirements and copyrightable subject matter. Copyright vests in an original work of authorship fixed in a tangible medium of expression. A broad range of subject matter may be eligible for copyright protection including literary works, music, sculptures, and art. Students should understand what subject matter can be protected under copyright law and why. This chapter summarizes the requirements for copyright protection and copyrightable subject matter in a way that will allow students to systematically identify the issues and apply the correct legal rules to most exam questions.

COPYRIGHT REQUIREMENTS AND COPYRIGHTABLE SUBJECT MATTER REVIEW

Requirements

Students should be familiar with three requirements for obtaining copyright protection. First, the subject matter must be an original work of authorship. Second, the work must be fixed in a tangible medium of expression. Third, although the modern trend is to construe them leniently, there are certain statutory formalities that copyright owners may need to observe to preserve their rights and remedies.[1] This section reviews these three requirements.

Originality

Copyright protection exists when there is an *original* work of *authorship* fixed in a *tangible* sense.[2] "Originality" means that (1) the

---

[1] 2 Nimmer on Copyright § 7.01 (2017).

[2] 17 U.S.C. § 102(a) (emphasis added).

work was independently created and (2) possesses at least some minimal degree of creativity.[3]

Independent Creation

A work is independently created so long as it was not copied and it is the product from the independent efforts of its author.[4] "Originality" has been distinguished from the "novelty" requirement in patent law, in that a work "will not be denied copyright protection simply because it is substantially similar to a work previously produced by others."[5] However, courts have acknowledged that there must be a "distinguishable variation" from an original work in order for the author to have produced anything that "owes origin to him."[6] For example, simply translating an original work into a different medium is considered a "trivial variation" that does not support a claim for copyright protection.[7]

Creativity

The amount of creativity required to satisfy the originality requirement is extremely low.[8] To be considered creative, the subject matter must bear a "spark of distinctiveness in copyrightable expression."[9]

Fixation

A work of authorship must be "fixed" in a tangible medium of expression to obtain copyright protection. Fixed means that one must be able to perceive, reproduce, or communicate the work for more than a transitory time period directly or with the aid of a device. A work is fixed in either a phonorecord or a copy. A phonorecord is a medium such as a CD or record in which only sounds are fixed. The statute recognizes the rapid development of storage technology by permitting a phonorecord to include material objects in which sounds are fixed by any method "later developed."[10] A copy is any medium other than a phonorecord such as a DVD or videotape. It is now well-settled that digital mediums such as computer memory and storage

---

[3] Feist Publ'ns, Inc. v. Rural Tel. Serv. Co., 499 U.S. 340, 345 (U.S. 1991).

[4] Mag Jewelry Co., Inc. v. Cherokee, Inc., 496 F.3d 108, 116 (1st Cir. 2007); Boisson v. Banian, Ltd., 273 F.3d 262, 270 (2d Cir. 2001).

[5] Berg v. Symons, 393 F. Supp. 2d 525, 541 (S.D. Tex. 2005).

[6] *See e.g.,* Burrow-Giles Lithographic Co. v. Sarony, 111 U.S. 53, 58 (1884).

[7] L. Batlin & Son, Inc. v. Snyder, 536 F. 2d 486, 491 (2d. Cir. 1976).

[8] *See e.g.,* Feist Publ'ns, Inc. v. Rural Tel. Serv. Co., 499 U.S. 340 (1990).

[9] 1 Nimmer on Copyright § 2.01[B] (2017).

[10] 17 U.S.C. § 101.

are also tangible mediums of expression.[11] A work that is being transmitted, such as a sporting event, is fixed in a tangible medium of expression if a simultaneous recording of the work is being made.[12]

Formalities

The Copyright Act of 1976 required that certain formalities be satisfied to preserve an author's rights in a copyrighted work. However, when the U.S. enacted the Berne Convention Implementation Act of 1988, it limited the significance of some formalities and in effect eliminated others. A detailed analysis of the current status of copyright formalities is beyond the scope of most IP survey courses. However, students should be familiar with the following traditional formalities: publication, notice, registration and submitting a deposit.

Publication

A work is published when it is made available to the general public with the owner's consent. Historically, the publication requirement stated that federal copyright protection was not triggered until the work was published. This is no longer true since copyright protection attaches once an original work of authorship is fixed in a tangible medium of expression. However, the definition of publication is still important as it may be used to determine other issues such as the length of the copyright term of works for hire or works owned by entities.

Notice

The notice requirement specifies that certain information such as the first year of publication, the name of the copyright holder, and the copyright symbol or the word "Copyright" be affixed to published copies of a work. Some form of the notice requirement applies to works published before March 1, 1989. For works published after the ratification of the Berne Convention notice is optional. However, having access to properly noticed copies eliminates an alleged infringer's innocent infringer defense.[13]

Registration

Registration is a voluntary requirement, but Congress provides certain incentives to owners that do register their works. For example, registering a work with the U.S. Copyright Office is prima facie evidence of a valid copyright. Also, if the work originated in the

---

[11] *See e.g.,* Stern Electronics v. Kaufman, 669 F.2d 852 (2d Cir. 1982); Midway Mfg. v. Arctic Int'l, 704 F.2d 1009 (7th Cir. 1983), *cert. denied,* 464 U.S. 823 (1983).

[12] 17 U.S.C. § 101 (2017).

[13] 17 U.S.C. § 401(d) (2017).

U.S. or a non-Berne country then in order for the owner to sue for copyright infringement in federal court, the allegedly infringed work must be registered with the U.S. Copyright Office. Further, owners of registered works are eligible to receive statutory damages and attorney fees.

Deposit

To enhance the collection of the Library of Congress, the Copyright Act requires two copies or phonorecords of a work published in the U.S. to be deposited with the U.S. Copyright Office within three months of its publication date.[14] While failure to make a deposit no longer results in forfeiture of copyright protection, it can delay the registration process and result in a $250 fine.

Categories of Eligible Subject Matter

U.S. Copyright law sets forth the following categories of eligible subject matter: (1) literary works, (2) musical works, (3) dramatic works, (4) pantomimes and choreographic works, (5) pictorial, graphic, and sculptural works, (6) motion pictures and other audiovisual works, (7) sound recordings, and (8) architectural works.[15]

Literary Works

Literary works are non-audiovisual works expressed in words, numbers or other indicia.[16] For example, literary works can take the form of books or periodicals.

Musical and Dramatic Works

Musical and Dramatic works are not defined in the statute as their definitions are self-explanatory. Musical works include all various genres of songs and lyrics. Dramatic works are stories related by narrative, dialogue or action.[17] Copyright protection for dramatic works also extends to the instructions for performing the work.

Pantomimes and Choreographic Works

A pantomime is a form of dramatic work consisting of movement or gesture without speech. A choreographic work is dance. Generally, pantomimes and choreographic works can be fixed in a tangible medium by special notation or by visual recording.

---

[14] 17 U.S.C. § 407 (2017).

[15] 17 U.S.C. § 102(a) (2017).

[16] 17 U.S.C. § 101 (2017).

[17] 1 Nimmer on Copyright § 2.06 (2017).

Pictorial, Graphic, and Sculptural Works

Examples of pictorial, graphic and sculptural works include "two-dimensional and three dimensional works of fine, graphic, and applied art, photographs, prints and art reproductions, maps, globes, charts, diagrams, models, and technical drawings, including architecture plans."[18]

Motion Pictures and Other Audiovisual Works

An audiovisual work consists "of a series of related images which are intrinsically intended to be shown by the use of machines, or devices such as projectors, viewers, or electronic equipment, together with accompanying sounds, if any."[19] A motion picture is a type of audiovisual work that imparts the impression of motion and includes any sounds (sound effects, music, dialogue, etc.) that accompany the visual images.[20] This category includes films and video games.

Sound Recordings

A sound recording is a fixation of a series of musical, spoken or other sounds. Sound recordings do not include sounds that accompany audiovisual works.[21]

Architectural Works

Non-functional elements of an original building design embodied in a drawing, the building itself, or any other tangible medium of expression is protectable under copyright law as an architectural work. In addition to only protecting nonfunctional elements, an existing copyright in the architecture of a building located in public will not restrict others from taking pictures of the building.[22]

Other Categories

In addition to the enumerated categories above, semiconductor and vessel hull designs are eligible for copyright protection. In addition, compilations, literary characters, and derivative works are also copyrightable. Derivative works are works created based on a preexisting work. Derivative works are summarized in Chapter 8. Compilations and literary characters are discussed below.

---

[18] 17 U.S.C. § 101 (2017).

[19] Id.

[20] Id.

[21] Id.

[22] *See e.g.,* Leicester v. Warner Bros., 232 F.3d 1212 (9th Cir. 2000).

Compilations and Collective Works

A compilation is created by assembling preexisting materials or information.[23] Even though a compilation may consist of facts, it is copyrightable because the information has been arranged in an original way. Collective works are a type of compilation. An author creates a collective work by assembling separate and independent works.[24] An anthology and encyclopedia are examples of collective works. Because a compilation includes preexisting materials, the copyright in a compilation extends solely to the material that was contributed by the author.[25] For example, the author of a work consisting of facts may obtain copyright protection in his original selection and arrangement of those facts.

Literary Characters

Fictional characters are eligible for copyright protection if they are sufficiently unique. For example, the character James Bond, created by Ian Fleming, has qualities that allow the character to be protected under copyright law.[26] The character is depicted in a specific way as cold blooded, overtly sexual, sophisticated, well-dressed, and prefers drinking martinis made in a certain way.[27] In contrast, a generic, private detective character would not be eligible for copyright protection.[28]

Limitations on Copyrightable Subject Matter

Certain subject matter is not protectable under copyright law. For example, works of the United States Federal Government, such as a federal district court legal opinion, are not eligible for copyright protection.[29] Works that have no creativity such as fragmentary words and short phrases such as names, titles, and slogans; familiar symbols or designs; typefaces or fonts, lettering or coloring; blank forms; and mere listing of ingredients or contents also receive no copyright protection.[30] This section will discuss additional doctrines that place limits on the copyright protection of certain subject matter.

---

[23] 17 U.S.C. § 101.

[24] Id.

[25] 17 U.S.C. § 103.

[26] *See e.g.,* Metro-Goldwyn-Mayer, Inc. v. Am. Honda Motor Co., 900 F. Supp. 1287 (C.D. Cal. 1995).

[27] Id.

[28] *See e.g.,* Warner Bros. Pictures v. CBS, 216 F.2d 945 (9th Cir. 1954).

[29] Note that 17 U.S.C. § 105 states that the Government may receive and hold copyrights that are transferred to it.

[30] 37 CFR § 202.1(a) (Other examples of works not subject to copyright are included in sections (b)–(e) of this Code).

Facts

A fact, whether alone or as part of a compilation, is not copyrightable.[31] Similarly, one who discovers a fact is not the "author" of that fact for the purpose of copyright.[32] However, an original compilation of facts can portray a sense of creativity based on the author's judgment in the order in which facts are placed and what facts are included.[33] Accordingly, the law may recognize a small amount of copyright protection for the original selection and arrangement of facts.

Ideas

Ideas, procedures, processes, systems, methods of operation, concepts, principles, or discoveries are not copyrightable.[34] For example, in *Baker v. Selden*, the U.S. Supreme Court held that a bookkeeping system that was described in a book was not protectable under copyright. Similarly, in *Lotus v. Borland*, the U.S. Court of Appeals for the First Circuit held that a menu command hierarchy for spreadsheet software was a "method of operation" and therefore unprotectable under 17 U.S.C. § 102(b). Thus, the law prevents copyright from being used to protect subject matter that is more appropriately protected as a patent and ensures that ideas remain in the public domain, free for others to use.

However, an author's expression of an idea may be copyrightable. A typical cookbook is an example of a work that may contain both protectable and unprotectable elements. The unprotectable elements will most likely include the list of ingredients, the cooking steps, and any generic arrangement of the recipes.[35] Protectable elements will generally include any art work, pictures, and expressive text that accompanies the recipes.

The Merger and Scènes à Faire Doctrines

The doctrines of merger and scènes à faire follow from the idea/expression dichotomy discussed above. Under the doctrine of merger, if an idea can only be expressed in a limited number of ways, the idea merges with an author's expression of that idea and is not eligible for copyright protection. For example, generic, written

---

[31] Feist Publ'ns, Inc. v. Rural Tel. Serv. Co., 499 U.S. 340, 349 (U.S. 1991).

[32] *See e.g.,* Miller v. Universal City Studios, Inc., 650 F.2d 1365 (5th Cir. 1981).

[33] *Id,* at 348–49.

[34] 17 U.S.C. § 102(b) (2017).

[35] *See e.g.,* Lapine v. Seinfeld, 92 U.S.P.Q. 2d 1428 (S.D.N.Y. 2009).

instructions for entering into a sweepstakes contest are not eligible for copyright protection under the merger doctrine.[36]

Similarly, the scènes à faire doctrine rejects copyright protection for "incidents, characters or settings" that are standard in works on a given topic.[37] For example, in a golf video game, common display elements such as a wind meter and a golf club selection feature would not be eligible for copyright protection because they are "indispensable to an accurate video representation of the game."[38]

The Useful Article Doctrine

A useful article is a utilitarian object. The useful article doctrine extends copyright protection to artistic elements or features of useful articles. Under the statute, a feature of a useful article is eligible for copyright protection only if (1) it can be perceived as a two- or three-dimensional work separate from the useful article and (2) is protectable as a pictorial, graphical or sculptural work if it were imagined separately from the useful article into which it is incorporated.[39] The Supreme Court's recent decision in *Star Athletica, LLC v. Varsity Brands* illustrates the application of this statute. There, the Supreme Court found that the lines, chevrons, and shapes on cheerleading uniforms were separable features eligible for copyright protection.[40]

COPYRIGHT SUBJECT MATTER CHECKLIST

With the above Review in mind, the Copyright Subject Matter Checklist is presented below.

A. **REQUIREMENTS.** Determine whether the necessary and optional requirements for copyright protection have been satisfied. A work must be original and fixed in a tangible medium of expression. Also consider whether certain statutory formalities have been satisfied.

    1. **Originality.** Is the work original? Originality requires independent creation and creativity. If the author produced the work without copying it from an existing work, it was

---

[36] *See e.g.,* Morrissey v. Proctor & Gamble, 379 F.2d 675 (1st Cir. 1967).

[37] Atari, Inc. v. N. Am. Phillips Consumer Elecs. Corp., 672 F.2d 607, 616 (7th Cir. 1982).

[38] Incredible Techs., Inc. v. Virtual Techs. Inc., 400 F.3d 1007, 1036 (7th Cir. 2005).

[39] Star Athletica, L.L.C. v. Varsity Brands, Inc., 137 S. Ct. 1002, 1005 (2017).

[40] Id. at 1008–1009.

created independently. The law requires an extremely low amount of creativity.

2. **Fixation.** Is the work fixed such that it can be perceived, produced or communicated? Media on which a work can be fixed includes a CD, a DVD, and computer memory. Live performances are not considered fixed unless they are simultaneously recorded.

3. **Formalities.** Has the owner satisfied the formality requirements for publication, notice, registration, or submitting a deposit? While failure to satisfy each formality is not fatal to a claim of copyright, the law incentivizes owners to adhere to the formality requirements.

    a. **Publication.** A work is published when it is made available to the general public with the owner's consent. Publication is no longer required for a work to be protected under U.S. Copyright law.

    b. **Notice.** This optional formality requires that (1) the first year of publication, (2) the name of the copyright holder, and (3) an indicia of copyright be affixed to a published copy of a work.

    c. **Registration.** Registration of a work with the U.S. Copyright Office creates an official government record of the copyrighted work. A work that originated in the U.S. must be registered in order for the owner to sue for copyright infringement in federal court.

    d. **Deposit.** This formality requires two copies of the work be submitted to the U.S. Copyright Office. Failure to make a deposit within three months of publication can slow registration and subject the owner to a fine.

B. **CATEGORIES OF ELIGIBLE SUBJECT MATTER.** How would you categorize the work? The U.S. Copyright statute lists several categories of copyright eligible subject matter. The statute provides definitions for some of the categories and leaves some self-explanatory categories undefined.

    1. **Literary Works.** Literary works are non-audiovisual works expressed in words, numbers or other indicia.

    2. **Musical Works.** Musical works are songs and song lyrics.

    3. **Dramatic Works.** Dramatic works are stories related by narrative, dialogue or action.

4.   **Pantomimes and Choreographic Works.** A pantomime is movement or gesture while a choreographic work is a dance.

5.   **Pictorial, Graphic, and Sculptural Works.** Commonly referred to as "PGS" works, these works include "two-dimensional and three-dimensional works of fine, graphic, and applied art, photographs, prints and art reproductions, maps, globes, charts, diagrams, models, and technical drawings, including architecture plans."[41]

6.   **Motion Pictures and Audiovisual Works.** An audiovisual work is a series of related images that may or may not be accompanied by sound. A motion picture is an audiovisual work that imparts the impression of motion and includes any sounds that accompany the visual images.

7.   **Sound Recordings.** A sound recording is a series of musical, spoken, or other sounds.

8.   **Architectural Works.** An architectural work includes the non-functional elements of an original building design embodied in a drawing, the building itself or any other tangible medium of expression.

9.   **Compilations and Collective Works.** A compilation is created by assembling preexisting materials or information. Collective works are a type of compilation and are a collection of separate works.

10. **Derivative Works.** Derivative works are works that are created based on a preexisting work.

11. **Other Categories.** Semiconductor and vessel hull designs are also eligible for copyright protection. Literary characters are also eligible for copyright protection if they are sufficiently unique.

C.   **LIMITATIONS ON COPYRIGHTABLE SUBJECT MATTER.** Consider whether any limiting doctrines will apply to the subject matter. A single work may contain both protectable expression and material that is not copyrightable. Identifying protectable expression is an exercise that is also important in analyzing a copyright infringement problem.

1.   **Facts.** A fact is not copyrightable. At best, an author may obtain thin copyright protection for how she expresses a

---

[41] 17 U.S.C. § 101 (2017).

fact. However, the fact itself cannot be protected and remains in the public domain.

2. **Ideas.** Is the subject matter merely an idea? Ideas are not copyrightable. Courts have extended this doctrine beyond ideas to include procedures, processes, systems, methods of operation, concepts, principles, and discoveries.

3. **The Merger Doctrine.** If an idea can only be expressed in a limited number of ways, the idea merges with an author's expression of that idea and is not eligible for copyright protection.

4. **The Scènes à Faire Doctrine.** Incidents, characters, and settings that are common in works of a certain genre are not copyrightable.

5. **The Useful Article Doctrine.** The useful article doctrine extends copyright protection to artistic features of utilitarian objects. A feature of a useful article is eligible for copyright protection only if (1) it can be perceived as a two- or three-dimensional work separate from the useful article and (2) is protectable as a pictorial, graphical or sculptural work if it were imagined separately from the useful article into which it is incorporated.[42]

ILLUSTRATIVE PROBLEMS

The two problems below illustrate how the Checklist can be used to resolve copyright subject matter questions.

■ **PROBLEM 7.1** ■

Chelsea is a comedian known throughout the country for her "lawyer" jokes. She is best known for her "you might be a lawyer if . . ." jokes. Examples of these jokes are:

—You might be a lawyer if . . .you have an IQ of 50 and they call you "Senator."

—You might be a lawyer if. . .accountants find you interesting.

—You might be a lawyer if . . . you think used car salesmen are honest people.

Chelsea has created thousands of lawyer jokes. She has compiled all the jokes into a published book called "You Might be a Lawyer If. . ." and claims ownership in the copyright and trademark rights

---

[42] Star Athletica, L.L.C. v. Varsity Brands, Inc., 137 S. Ct. 1002, 1005 (2017).

related to the jokes. Chelsea's book was published in October of 2015 and is properly registered with the United States Copyright Office. In addition, she performs a standup act several times a year that incorporates her lawyer jokes. She also sells merchandise such as cups and hats with lawyer jokes on them.

In several interviews promoting her book, Chelsea explained that she incorporated ideas for lawyer jokes from her fans, family, and friends into the jokes included in her book.

"I always get great ideas from the fans at my shows," she said. "About fifty percent of the jokes in the book are based on someone else's negative view of lawyers. But, to make them work comedically, I have to put them in my own words. The art is to condense an encounter with a lawyer into one funny sentence."

In February of 2016, Chelsea became aware that Jeff was selling t-shirts with exact copies of Chelsea's jokes. Chelsea contacted Jeff and informed him that she believed his selling of the t-shirts violated her copyright in the jokes. Jeff acknowledges that he copied jokes in Chelsea's book verbatim. However, Jeff asserts that the lawyer jokes in the book are not original to Chelsea and she therefore cannot claim copyright in the jokes. Chelsea sues Jeff for copyright infringement.

Discuss whether Chelsea has a valid copyright in her jokes.

Analysis

In order to prove copyright infringement, a plaintiff must show that she is the owner of a valid copyright and that the copyrighted work was copied by the defendant. Chapter 8 summarizes the law on copyright infringement. This question asks students to analyze the threshold issue of whether Chelsea has a valid copyright in her lawyer jokes.

Facts and ideas are not copyrightable because they lack originality. However, the original expression of an idea is copyrightable. An original work is a work that is independently created by the author and possesses a minimal degree of creativity. The level of creativity required is extremely low.

Jeff is claiming that the subject matter, lawyer jokes, are not copyrightable. However, copyright protects the expression of the author, not the subject matter. Here, there is evidence that the jokes in Chelsea's books are her protected expression. In her interview, Chelsea explained that even though all the joke ideas do not originate with her, she must use her own words to form the comedic jokes included in the book. Chelsea's statements, if true, establish that the jokes included in her book are her original expression. Thus, Chelsea has a strong argument that she possesses a valid copyright in the jokes in her book.

■ PROBLEM 7.2 ■

New Look, Inc. ("New Look") is a designer and manufacturer of children's clothing. New Look makes animal-themed hooded sweatshirts ("hoodies") which have sculpted hoods. The sculpted hoods take the form of the head of a stuffed animal. The head includes features such as stuffed ears, whiskers, eyes, and a mouth or beak. New Look also includes elements that create paws at the end of the sleeves of the hoodie. The wearer of the hoodie can attach their hands to the paw elements via an elastic strap. New Look has obtained registered copyrights in all its designs.

Claw Creations, Ltd. ("Claw") is a competing clothing brand. Claw also makes a line of animal-themed hoodies for children.

In November of 2016, New Look filed suit, asserting that Claw infringed its copyright by copying three of it animal hoodie designs that invoke a bear, lion, and an owl. In its defense, Claw plans to argue that New Look's designs are useful articles and therefore ineligible for copyright protection.

Discuss the merits of Claw's defense.

Analysis

Problem 8.2 requires you to apply the useful article doctrine.

The starting point for analysis of a copyright infringement problem is whether the plaintiff owns a valid copyright in eligible subject matter. Original works of authorship that are fixed in a tangible medium of expression are eligible for copyright protection. Pictorial, graphic, and sculptural ("PGS") works are works of authorship and include "two-dimensional and three-dimensional works of fine, graphic, and applied art, photographs, prints and art reproductions, maps, globes, charts, diagrams, models, and technical drawings, including architectural plans."[43]

PGS works may be incorporated into useful articles. Useful articles are articles that have a useful function "that is not merely to portray the appearance of the article or to convey information."[44] The design of a useful article may be eligible for copyright protection if it has PGS "features that can be identified separately from, and are capable of existing independently of, the utilitarian aspects of the

---

[43] 17 U.S.C. § 101 (2017).
[44] Id.

article."[45] The two-part test under the useful article doctrine requires first, a determination of whether the feature in question "can be perceived as a two-or three-dimensional work of art separate from the useful article."[46] Second, the decision maker must determine whether the feature at issue "would qualify as a protectable pictorial, graphic, or sculptural work—either on its own or fixed in some other tangible medium of expression—if it were imagined separately from the useful article into which it is incorporated."[47]

Here, New Look's hoodies are useful articles because they serve a useful function as clothing. The issue is whether the sculpted head and paw designs of New Look's hoodies are eligible for copyright protection. Specifically, whether the designs can be identified separately and are capable of existing independently from the hoodie itself.

First, New Look's hoodies have two-and three-dimensional features that appear to have PGS qualities separate from the hoodie itself. The hood contains elements such as stuffed ears, whiskers, and an animal mouth. In addition, the end of the sleeves contain paw designs. These features could be removed from the hoodie and the hoodie would still function as an article of clothing. Thus, New Look's separable features satisfy the first requirement for copyright eligibility.

Second, the animal features of New Look's hoodies can exist separately from the hoodie as protectable PGS works. The ears, paws, nose, and mouth are two-or three-dimensional sculptural or graphic works. Further, imaginatively removing these features from the hoodie and applying them to another medium, such as other clothing or a canvas, would not replicate the hoodie itself. Therefore, New Look's features satisfy the second requirement for copyright eligibility.

In sum, it is likely that Claw's argument that New Look's hoodies are ineligible for copyright protection will fail.

POINTS TO REMEMBER

- Originality in copyright law is different from the novelty requirement in patent law. Two works that are independently created and are substantially similar may both be eligible for copyright protection.

---

[45] Id.

[46] Star Athletic, L.L.C. v. Varsity Brands, Inc. 137 S. Ct. 1002, 1007 (2017).

[47] Id.

- A work of authorship must be "fixed" in a tangible medium of expression to obtain copyright protection. "Fixed" means that one must be able to perceive, reproduce, or communicate the work for more than a transitory time period directly or with the aid of a device.

- A work is considered published when it is made available to the general public with the owner's consent.

- Registration is a voluntary requirement, but Congress provides certain incentives to owners that register their works. Registering a work with the U.S. Copyright Office is prima facie evidence of a valid copyright. Also, owners of registered works are eligible to receive statutory damages and attorney fees.

- Ideas and facts by themselves are not eligible for copyright protection. However, an author's original expression of facts or ideas is copyrightable.

CHAPTER 8

Copyright Ownership, Rights, and Infringement

T he owner of a valid copyright has several rights, including the right to perform, distribute or make copies of a copyrighted work. Copyright infringement occurs when these rights are violated. For example, a party who makes an unauthorized copy of a copyrighted work is liable for copyright infringement. Students must know how to identify protected expression under copyright law and then understand how to determine whether that protected expression is infringed. This chapter will summarize the law concerning copyright ownership, rights and infringement.

COPYRIGHT OWNERSHIP, RIGHTS, AND INFRINGEMENT REVIEW

Duration

A work's copyright term is based on several factors including its publication date and authorship.[1] With each new copyright act, the term for protection has increased. Thus, a work's copyright duration depends in part on the applicable law as of its publication date. A detailed analysis of the duration of copyright protection for works published at different time periods is beyond the scope of this book.

Students should at least understand how the law would apply to works published in the last decade. Current law states that a copyright in a work published in the U.S. after 2002 will expire after the life of the author plus 70 years. If the author is anonymous, pseudonymous, or the work is a work made for hire, the copyright term lasts 95 years from the date of publication or 120 years from creation, whichever is less. The same duration rules above apply to sound recordings first published in the U.S. after March 1, 1989, and architectural works first published in the U.S. after Dec. 1, 1990.

---

[1] *See* 17 U.S.C. §§ 301–305 (2017).

Copyright in an unpublished work will expire after the life of the author plus 70 years. If the author is anonymous, pseudonymous, her death date is not known, or the work is a work made for hire the copyright term for an unpublished work lasts 120 years from the creation of the work.

Ownership

The author or authors of a work are the initial owners of the copyright in that work.[2]

A Joint Work

A joint work is a work prepared by two or more authors. If the authors all (1) contribute expression that is eligible for copyright protection and (2) intend that their individual contributions be merged in some way into a unitary whole, then the work in question is considered a joint work. Each joint author is a co-owner of the work and owns an undivided share in the work.[3] Generally, absent permission from the other joint author(s), a joint author may exercise her rights in the copyrighted work. However, all joint authors must agree to grant an exclusive license or assign the rights in the work to a third party.

A Work Made for Hire

If a work is made for hire then the law considers the employer or person that the work was made for the author of the work.[4] The employer or the person that the work was made for have all rights comprised in the copyright. There are two ways of creating a work made for hire. First, where the parties involved have expressly agreed in a written instrument, a work for hire is a work commissioned for use as a contribution to a "collective work, as a part of a motion picture or other audiovisual work, as a translation, as a supplementary work, as a compilation, as a test, as answer material for a test or as an atlas."[5] Second, a work made for hire is a work prepared by an employee within the scope of her employment.

A common issue in this area is determining whether a person prepared a work in question in the scope of their employment or as an independent contractor. If a party prepares a work as an independent contractor, absent an agreement to the contrary, the work is not a work made for hire. To determine whether a work was prepared within the scope of a person's employment, the Supreme

---

[2] 17 U.S.C. § 201(a) (2017).

[3] Id.

[4] 17 U.S.C. § 201(b) (2017).

[5] 17 U.S.C. § 101 (2017).

Court set forth several factors to consider in *Community for Creative Non-Violence (CCNV) v. Reid*. The factors to be considered are: (1) the hiring party's right to control the manner and means by which the work is done, (2) the skill required, (3) the source of the instrumentalities and tools, (4) the location of the work, (5) the duration of the relationship between the parties, (6) whether the hiring party has the right to assign additional projects to the hired party, (7) the extension of the hired party's discretion over when and how long to work, (8) the method of payment, (9) the hired party's role in hiring and paying assistants, (10) whether the work is part of the regular business of the hiring party, (11) whether the hiring party is in business, (12) the provision of employee benefits, and (13) the tax treatment of the hired party.[6]

Rights

Generally, a copyright owner has the right to reproduce, distribute, perform or display her work, create derivative works, and prevent unauthorized copying of her work. This section summarizes the most common rights covered in an IP survey course.

Derivative Works

A copyright owner has the exclusive right to prepare derivative works based on her preexisting work. A derivate work is eligible for copyright protection if it recasts, transforms or adapts a preexisting copyrighted work and contributes new, original expression to the preexisting work.[7] A sequel to a preexisting motion picture or book is an example of a derivative work. Additional examples of derivative works include a translation, musical arrangement, dramatization, fictionalization, sound recording, art reproduction, abridgment, a condensation, and a work consisting of editorial revisions, annotations, elaborations or other modifications that as a whole represent an original work of authorship.[8]

Public Distribution

The owner of a copyright in a work has the right to distribute copies of the copyrighted work to the public. Distribution may occur in various ways including sale, rental, lease or lending.[9] The first sale doctrine limits the public distribution right by permitting an owner of a lawful copy of a work to sell or dispose of that copy without the

---

[6] Cmty. for Creative Non-Violence v. Reid, 490 U.S. 730, 751 (1989).

[7] *But see* Anderson v. Stallone, 11 U.S.P.Q. 2d (BNA) 1161, 1169 (C.D. Cal. 1989) (holding that an author who creates a derivative work without permission cannot claim copyright in the derivative work).

[8] 17 U.S.C. § 101 (2017).

[9] 17 U.S.C. § 106(3) (2017).

copyright owner's authorization.[10] The first sale doctrine also applies to copies of a copyrighted work lawfully made abroad and then sold in the United States.[11]

Public Performance

An owner of a copyright in a literary, musical, dramatic, choreographic work, pantomime, motion picture and other audiovisual work has the right to perform the work publicly.[12] Performing a work means to "recite, rendering, play, dance, or act it, either directly or by means of any device or process or, in the case of a motion picture or other audiovisual work, to show its images in any sequence or to make the sounds accompanying it audible."[13] A copyright holder's public performance rights are limited by the public interest exemptions listed in 17 U.S.C. § 110. In addition, a third party may obtain a license from the copyright owner to perform the copyrighted work or a statutory compulsory license.[14]

Public Display

A copyright owner has the right to publicly display "literary, musical, dramatic, and choreographic works, pantomimes, and pictorial, graphic, or sculptural works, including the individual images of a motion picture or other audiovisual work."[15] A work is displayed if it shown to the public directly or via some other means. Under a statutory exception, owners of a lawfully made copy of the work may publicly display the copy of the work to viewers at the place where the copy is located.[16]

Moral Rights

Moral rights stem from the belief that a work is an extension of the personality of the author. While moral rights enjoy broad recognition in other countries, the right is limited in the U.S. Moral rights protect the author of a visual art from false attribution, intentional modifications to the work which would be prejudicial to the author's honor or reputation such as mutilation or distortion, and destruction of the work if it is of a recognized stature. Visual art is narrowly defined as a painting, drawing, print, sculpture or still photographic image produced only for exhibition purposes that exist

---

[10] *But see* 17 U.S.C. § 109(b) (2017) (the first sale doctrine does not apply to records or software rentals).

[11] *See e.g.,* Kirtsaeng v. John Wiley & Sons, Inc., 568 U.S. 519 (2013).

[12] 17 U.S.C. § 106(4) (2017).

[13] 17 U.S.C. § 101 (2017).

[14] *See e.g.,* 17 U.S.C. §§ 111, 116, 118–119 (2017).

[15] 17 U.S.C. § 106(5) (2017).

[16] 17 U.S.C. § 109(c) (2017).

in limited quantities.[17] A work made for hire is not a visual art for the purposes of the statute. Moral rights are not transferable but may be waived by a written agreement.

Copyright Infringement

A violation of any exclusive right (e.g., reproduction, distribution, public performance, display, etc.) of a copyright holder is copyright infringement. The first element of any copyright infringement claim is that a plaintiff must own a valid copyright in the alleged infringed work.[18] Next, a plaintiff must show that her protected expression was derived or actually copied by the defendant which resulted in the alleged infringing work having a substantial similarity to the plaintiff's work.

Copying

Actual copying refers to the act of the defendant copying the original work. Based on a preponderance of the evidence, the fact-finder determines whether the defendant copied the plaintiff's work. Actual copying can be shown by (1) direct evidence such as an admission or testimony, or (2) inferred from evidence that the defendant had access to the original work and that the alleged infringing work is probatively similar to the original work, or (3) inferred in the absence of evidence of access, if the original work and the alleged infringing work are strikingly similar. IP survey students will rarely be asked about legal disputes in which there is direct evidence of actual copying. Thus, students should have a working understanding of the other ways in which actual copying may be established.

Actual copying can be established by evidence of access and probative similarity. The most used test to evaluate whether copying has occurred is the sliding scale framework articulated in *Arnstein v. Porter*.[19] At one extreme, if there are no similarities between the plaintiff's work and the alleged infringing work, then the plaintiff cannot prove copying. At the other extreme, if there is no evidence that the alleged infringer had access to the plaintiff's work, then the similarities between the works must be striking. In the middle, where there is evidence of access and the existence of similarities, the fact-finder must determine whether the similarities are sufficient to show copying.

Since, most copyright exam questions will assume evidence of both access and similarity, analyzing the access and probative

---

[17] 17 U.S.C. § 101 (2017).

[18] Feist Publ'ns, Inc. v. Rural Tel. Serv. Co., 499 U.S. 340, 361 (1991).

[19] *See* Arnstein v. Porter, 154 F.2d 464 (2d Cir. 1946).

similarity elements are key to understanding copyright infringement analysis. To establish access, the copyright owner must show that the defendant had a reasonable opportunity to experience the plaintiff's work. For example, a defendant will likely have access to a work that is widely disseminated to the public. A defendant may also be found to have access to a work that is sent to a third party with which the defendant has a close relationship.

Two works satisfy the probative similarity test if a fact-finder could infer from the evidence that one was copied from the other. For example, two works that have the same typographical errors may be evidence of copying.

In the absence of evidence of access, the similarities between the two works must be strikingly similar to prove copying. To show that two works are strikingly similar, similarities between two works must appear in a sufficiently unique and complex context.

Improper Appropriation of Protected Expression

Identifying Protected Expression

Copyright infringement requires that a defendant copy protected expression of the original work and the that the intended audience of the work deem the protected expression substantially similar. In order to identify the protected expression, the plaintiff's work is separated into elements. The decision maker evaluates each element to determine whether it is protectable. The decision maker filters out the unprotectable elements leaving only the protected expression. If the work at issue is a story, for example, the filtering step will eliminate ideas, generic plot points, generic character attributes, and elements that could be considered unprotectable under the scènes à faire doctrine.[20] The fact-finder then compares the protected expression to the alleged infringing work from the viewpoint of an ordinary observer to determine whether they are substantially similar.

The Second Circuit adopted a similar process for determining infringement of computer software referred to as the abstraction, filtration, comparison test.[21] Under this test, the abstraction step separates the elements of the software. Elements at the highest level of abstraction will be afforded no protection, some elements will have limited protection, and elements at the lowest level of abstraction (e.g., object code) will be fully protected. The filtration step filters out the elements of the software that are unprotected by copyright. In software, the elements that are not protected are generally elements

---

[20] *See e.g.,* Nichols v. Universal Pictures Corp., 45 F.2d 119 (2d Cir. 1930).

[21] Comput. Assocs. Int'l v. Altai, 982 F.2d 693, 706 (2d Cir. 1992).

that are dictated by computer functionality. Finally, during the comparison step, the fact-finder compares the remaining protected elements of the plaintiff's work to the allegedly infringing work.

Comparing the Protected Expression to the Alleged Infringing Work

To determine whether there is a substantial similarity between the protectable elements of an original work and the alleged infringing work, a fact-finder must consider the type of people that find the works similar, the nature of the similarity, and how substantial similarity is measured. Concerning the nature of the similarity, the fact-finder must consider whether the works are similar as a whole (e.g., the selection and arrangement of plot points in a fictional story) or if there is a substantial similarity between the alleged infringing work and a protectable element of the plaintiff's work. Substantial similarity is measured based on the expression in question. A greater degree of similarity is required for ideas that have limited ways of being expressed. Conversely, less similarity is required for ideas that can be expressed in many ways.

A Note on the *de minimis* Doctrine

The *de minimis* doctrine states that the copying of a small and insignificant portion of a work is not copyright infringement. However, the *de minimis* doctrine does not apply to music sampling. Sampling, a technique often used in popular music, is the copying of musical notes or beats from another's song. Creating an unauthorized, two-second sample of a song is copyright infringement.[22]

Indirect Infringement

Generally

Liability for indirect copyright infringement is generally governed by common law tort liability principles. For there to be liability for indirect infringement, there must be direct infringement of the copyrighted work. A third party may be vicariously liable for copyright infringement if the third party has a right to supervise the direct infringer and a financial interest in the infringing activity. For example, the owner of a theater venue is vicariously liable for the performance of infringing works in the venue. If a third party induces or causes another to infringe a copyrighted work, the third party is liable for contributory infringement. As an illustration, a third party that lends a lawful copy of a DVD to a friend, knowing that the friend will make infringing copies of the DVD is a contributory infringer.

---

[22] *Bridgeport Music, Inc. v. Dimension Films*, 410 F.3d 792, 800 (6th Cir. 2005).

Dual use technology can also be the subject of indirect copyright infringement lawsuits and is discussed below.

Duel Use Technologies

Dual use technology refers to products that are capable of being used for infringing activity but also have substantial non-infringing uses. An early example of dual use technology is the VTR or VCR. This technology could be used for non-infringing activities such as viewing a lawfully obtained copy of a movie or for infringing uses such as making unlawful copies of a television program for sale or distribution.

The sale of a product that may be used to make infringing copies of a copyrighted work does not constitute contributory infringement if the product in question has legitimate and unobjectionable purposes.[23] In *Sony Corp. Of Am. v. Universal Studios, Inc.*, the Supreme Court held that Sony was not liable for contributory infringement by selling VTRs. MGM and other copyright holders argued that the VTR could be used to make infringing copies of films and TV shows sold on video cassette. The Supreme Court found that the VTR had legitimate purposes such as allowing consumers to make their own videos and also providing consumers with the flexibility to enjoy television programming on their own schedule, i.e., time-shifting.

The digital age has ushered in an era of dual use software platforms. Generally, an entity that markets and sells a dual use product is not liable for indirect infringement. However, an entity that takes active steps to encourage infringing activities may be liable for inducing infringement.[24] In *MGM Studios Inc. v. Grokster*, the defendant companies Grokster and Streamcast took steps to convert users of the defunct Napster file sharing service to their platforms. Napster was a popular file sharing software platform that was crippled by lawsuits because its users engaged in rampant copyright infringing activities. In reaching its determination that Grokster was liable for induced infringement, the Supreme Court noted that there was evidence to suggest that Grokster and Streamcast sought to replace Napster and encouraged users to download copyrighted work without authorization.

---

[23] *See e.g.,* Sony Corp. of Am. v. Universal City Studios, Inc., 464 U.S. 417 (1984), *superseded by statute*, Digital Millenium Copyright Act of 1998, Pub. L. No. 115–64.

[24] *See e.g.,* MGM Studios Inc. v. Grokster, Ltd., 545 U.S. 913 (2005).

COPYRIGHT OWNERSHIP, RIGHTS, AND INFRINGEMENT CHECKLIST

With the above Review in mind, the Copyright Ownership, Rights, and Infringement Checklist is presented below.

A. DURATION. Determine the duration of a work's copyright term. The term varies based on a number of factors including the type of work,[25] authorship, and whether the work was published. Further, the applicable term may depend on when the work was created or published. The law as it would apply to works published today is summarized below.

    1. Generally. A copyright in a work published in the U.S. will expire after the life of the author plus 70 years.

    2. Anonymous, Pseudonymous, or the Work Is a Work Made for Hire. For a work of this type published after 2002, the copyright term lasts 95 years from the date of publication or 120 years from creation, whichever is less.

    3. Unpublished Work, Generally. Copyright in an unpublished work will expire after the life of the author plus 70 years.

    4. Unpublished Works Where the Author Is Anonymous, Pseudonymous, Her Death Date Is Not Known, or the Work Is a Work Made for Hire. The copyright term lasts 120 years from creation of the work.

B. OWNERSHIP. Determine who or what has ownership rights in the copyrighted work. Ownership may depend on who created the work and the facts that led to its creation.

    1. Authors and Ownership. Absent an agreement or obligation to the contrary, ownership of a copyrighted work vests in its author.

    2. A Joint Work. A work is a joint work if two or more authors contributed copyrightable expression to the work and intended that their individual contributions be merged to create the unitary work. Each author of a joint work is a co-owner and generally owns an undivided interest in the whole work.

---

[25] Points 1 and 2 below apply to sound recordings first published in the U.S. after March 1, 1989, and architectural works first published in the U.S. after December 1, 1990.

3. **A Work Made for Hire.** A work made for hire is not owned by the author. Instead, a work made for hire is owned by the person or entity that the work was made for. Generally, a work made for hire can be commissioned or made by an employee within the scope of their employment.

    a. **Commissioned.** Where the parties involved have expressly agreed in a written instrument, a work for hire is a work commissioned for use as a contribution to a "collective work, as a part of a motion picture or other audiovisual work, as a translation, as a supplementary work, as a compilation, as a test, as answer material for a test or as and atlas."[26]

    b. **Within the Scope of Their Employment.** Was the work prepared by an employee within the scope of their employment? If so, then the work in question is a work for hire and owned by the employer. In some instances, it may be necessary to use the *Reid* factors to determine whether the creator is an "employee."[27] The factors to be considered are:

        (1) the hiring party's right to control the manner and means by which the work is done, (2) the skill required, (3) the source of the instrumentalities and tools, (4) the location of the work, (5) the duration of the relationship between the parties, (6) whether the hiring party has the right to assign additional projects to the hired party, (7) the extension of the hired party's discretion over when and how long to work, (8) the method of payment, (9) the hired party's role in hiring and paying assistants, (10) whether the work is part of the regular business of the hiring party, (11) whether the hiring party is in business, (12) the provision of employee benefits, and (13) the tax treatment of the hired party.

C. **RIGHTS.** Generally, the owner of a copyrighted work has the exclusive right to reproduce, distribute, perform or display his work, create derivative works, and prevent unauthorized copying of his work. Where applicable, students should take note of the doctrinal and statutory limitations placed on each right.

    1. **Derivative Works.** A derivative work is a work that is prepared based on a preexisting work. A copyright owner has the right to create derivative works based on his preexisting work. A derivative work is eligible for copyright

---

[26] 17 U.S.C. § 101 (2017).

[27] Cmty. for Creative Non-Violence v. Reid, 490 U.S. 730, 751 (1989).

protection if it contributes new and original expression to the preexisting work.

2. **Public Distribution.** This right permits the copyright owner to distribute copies of the copyrighted work to the public. The right is limited by the first sale doctrine which permits the owner of a lawful copy of a copyrighted work to sell that copy without the copyright owner's permission.

3. **Public Performance.** The public performance right gives the copyright owner the right to publicly perform a copyrighted work. This right is limited by several public interest exemptions.[28]

4. **Public Display.** A copyright owner has the right to display the copyrighted work in public. An exception in 17 U.S.C. § 109(c) permits owners of a lawfully made copy of the work to publicly display the copy of the work to viewers at the place where the copy is located.

5. **Moral Rights.** U.S. law recognizes moral rights in visual art. The right allows the author of a work to prohibit false attribution, intentional modifications and in some instances destruction of her work. In addition to being limited to visual art, the statute specifies that a work made for hire is not visual art.

D. **COPYRIGHT INFRINGEMENT.** Determine whether the copyright holder's rights have been infringed. First, the plaintiff must own a valid copyright in the original work. Next, the plaintiff must prove that the alleged infringing work is substantially similar to the plaintiff's work and resulted from the defendant copying or deriving the protected expression of the plaintiff's work.

1. **Copying.** Actual copying can be shown in several ways.

   a. **Direct Evidence.** Direct evidence such as an admission or testimony can be used to prove copying.

   b. **The Sliding Scale Test.** Apply the sliding scale test considering access and similarity.

      i. **No Similarities.** If there are no similarities between the two works then the plaintiff cannot prove copying.

      ii. **Access and Similarity.** Where there is evidence of access and the existence of similarities, the fact-

---

[28] 17 U.S.C. § 110 (2017).

finder must determine whether the similarities between the original work and the alleged infringing work are sufficient to show copying.

    iii. **Striking Similarity.** If there is no evidence of access then the similarities between the works must be striking.

  c. **Evidence of Striking Similarity.** Two works are strikingly similar if the similarities between the two works appear in a unique and complex context.

2. **Improper Appropriation of Protected Expression.** Determine whether the copied subject matter is protectable expression.

  a. **Identifying Protected Expression.** Examine the plaintiff's work and filter out unprotectable elements to identify copyrightable expression.

  b. **Comparing the Protected Expression to the Alleged Infringing Work.** Compare the protected expression to the alleged infringing work from the viewpoint of an ordinary observer to determine whether they are substantially similar.

  c. **The *de minimis* Doctrine.** The copying of a small and insignificant portion of a work is not copyright infringement. However, the *de minims* doctrine does not apply to music sampling.

3. **Indirect Infringement.** Liability for indirect infringement is predicated on a finding of direct infringement.

  a. **Vicarious Liability.** If a third party has a right to supervise the direct infringer and a financial interest in the infringing activity, they may be liable for indirect infringement.

  b. **Contributory Infringement.** If a third party induces or causes another to infringe a copyrighted work they are liable for contributory infringement.

  c. **Dual Use Technology.** The sale of dual use technology that is used to produce infringing copies of a copyrighted work does not constitute copyright infringement if the technology has a legitimate non-infringing purpose.

ILLUSTRATIVE PROBLEMS

Here are two problems that illustrate how the Checklist can be used to resolve copyright ownership, rights and infringement questions.

■ PROBLEM 8.1 ■

The Singer Group ("Singer") publishes insurance manuals. In 2006, David Dunner began working for Singer. Singer hired Dunner to write an insurance manual. Singer provided Dunner with an office at its headquarters and paid Dunner a salary of $3000 a month.

Dunner asserts that he entered into an oral agreement with Singer that Dunner and Singer would be co-owners of the manual and co-own the copyright in the manual. Dunner completed work on the manual in 2008. The manual was titled, "2008 Health Insurance."

That same year, Singer filed a copyright registration for "2008 Health Insurance." The registration indicated that the manual was a "work made for hire" and listed the Singer Group as the sole author.

Dunner worked for Singer as an officer and vice president of the corporation until 2012. After Dunner left Singer, he copied substantial portions of 2008 Health Insurance to create his own text called "Health Insurance Now." After discovering Health Insurance Now, Singer sued Dunner in federal court for copyright infringement.

Discuss whether Singer has a valid copyright in "2008 Health Insurance."

Analysis

To prevail in a copyright infringement suit, the plaintiff must show that he owns a valid copyright in the work and that the defendant made an unauthorized copy of the protected expression contained in the work. Here, the facts state that Dunner copied substantial portions of "2008 Health Insurance" to create Health Insurance Now. Accordingly, the determinative issue is whether Singer has a valid copyright in "2008 Health Insurance."

Generally, copyright protection attaches to the author of a work. However, if a work is made for hire, then the employer or the person the work was made for is the author of the work and the owner of the copyright, unless the parties have agreed otherwise in a signed instrument. A work is a "work made for hire" if it is prepared by an employee in the scope of their employment.

The facts indicate that Singer and Dunner did not sign a written agreement concerning the authorship or copyright ownership of

"2008 Health Insurance." Thus, the question is whether Dunner authored "2008 Health Insurance" while an employee of Singer, and did so in the scope of his employment.

To make this determination, students should apply the *Reid* factors. The factors to be considered are: (1) the hiring party's right to control the manner and means by which the work is done, (2) the skill required, (3) the source of the instrumentalities and tools, (4) the location of the work, (5) the duration of the relationship between the parties, (6) whether the hiring party has the right to assign additional projects to the hired party, (7) the extension of the hired party's discretion over when and how long to work, (8) the method of payment, (9) the hired party's role in hiring and paying assistants, (10) whether the work is part of the regular business of the hiring party, (11) whether the hiring party is in business, (12) the provision of employee benefits, and (13) the tax treatment of the hired party.[29]

Dunner's argument that Singer does not have a valid copyright in "2008 Health Insurance" will fail. Analyzing the facts using the *Reid* factors, it is clear that Dunner was an employee of Singer and wrote "2008 Health Insurance" within the scope of his employment. Singer is in the business of publishing insurance manuals. Singer hired Dunner to write an insurance manual which was part of Singer's regular business. The location of the work was Singer's headquarters. Singer also paid Dunner a regular salary. Further, the nature and length of the relationship between Dunner and Singer seems to weigh in favor of Dunner being an employee. Thus, "2008 Health Insurance" is a work made for hire and Singer is the owner of the copyright in "2008 Health Insurance."

■ PROBLEM 8.2 ■

Tableware, Inc. ("Tableware") manufactures and distributes casual dinnerware. In 2001, Tableware manufactured and sold a "Kitchen Basics" set in the U.S. that included four plates, four bowls, and four cups. Tableware designed the box for packaging the Kitchen Basics product. The design included the words "Kitchen Basics" printed in bold black letters on the long sides of the rectangular packaging and an overhead photograph of a circular table set with the contents of the package—four plates, four bowls, and four cups. In the lower right corner of the box the words "FOR *(4) PLATES, BOWLS, AND CUPS*" are printed in italicized lettering. In 2002, Tableware applied for and obtained a Certificate of Registration for the "Kitchen Basics" box design from the United States Copyright

---

[29] Cmty. for Creative Non-Violence v. Reid, 490 U.S. 730, 751 (1989).

Office. Due to budgeting concerns, Tableware was unable to correct the misspelling of the word "FOR" on its packaging until 2004.

Casual Cups ("Casual") is also a manufacturer and distributor of casual dinnerware. From 1991 to 2002, Casual specialized in selling cups and mugs. In 2003, Casual decided to sell a dinnerware set that included four plates, four bowls, and four cups. Since it was Casual's first time selling a product other than cups or mugs, Casual's design team purchased several of Tableware's "Kitchen Basics" sets to use the packaging as a model. Casual's final design included the words "Casual Kitchen" printed in bold black letters on the long sides of the rectangular packaging and an overhead photograph, similar to Tableware's, of a circular table set with the contents of the package—four plates, four bowls, and four cups. In the lower right corner of the box, the words "FOR *(4) PLATES, BOWLS, AND CUPS*" are printed in italicized lettering.

In late 2003, Casual began selling its dinnerware set in U.S. stores. In early 2004, Tableware executives became aware of Casual's "Casual Kitchen" product. Tableware sues Casual for infringing its copyright in its box design. Casual admits to purchasing and using the Tableware product as design inspiration but denies copying.

Discuss.

Analysis

To succeed in a suit for copyright infringement, a plaintiff must demonstrate that they are the owner of a valid copyright and that her protected expression was derived or actually copied by the defendant, which resulted in the alleged infringing work having a substantial similarity to the plaintiff's work. The second prong requires evidence of actual copying and a showing that so much of the plaintiff's protected expression was copied that it constitutes improper appropriation.

First, Tableware must show that it has a valid copyright in its box design. A copyright registration certificate is prima facie evidence of ownership of a valid copyright. Tableware received a Certificate for Registration on its design in 2002. Further, under the facts given, there seems to be no reason to question Tableware's copyright ownership. Thus, it is likely that Tableware has a valid copyright in its packaging design.

Next, Tableware must show that its protected expression was derived or actually copied by Casual which resulted in Casual's box design having a substantial similarity to Tableware's box design. This is a two-step process. First, Tableware must show that Casual actually copied its box design.

Actual copying can be shown by (1) direct evidence such as an admission or testimony, or (2) inferred from evidence that the defendant had access to the original work and that the alleged infringing work is probatively similar to the original work or (3) inferred in the absence of evidence of access if the original work and the alleged infringing work are strikingly similar.

Here, there is no direct evidence of copying but Casual conceded that it had access to the "Kitchen Basics" box design. There is also evidence of probative similarity between the two boxes. Both boxes include the brand names printed in bold black letters on the long sides of the rectangular packaging. Both boxes include an overhead photograph of a circular table set with the contents of the package—four plates, four bowls, and four cups. Finally, both boxes include the words "FOR (4) PLATES, BOWLS, AND CUPS" in italicized lettering printed in the lower right corner of the box. Moreover, Casual's box includes the misspelling of the word "FOR." Given the similarities, it is likely that Tableware will be able to show that Casual's box design is probatively similar to its "Kitchen Basics" box design.

Second, Tableware must show that Casual copied so much of the protectable elements of Tableware's box design that it constitutes improper appropriation. Students must first determine which elements of Tableware's box design are protected expression.

Here, the overhead photograph has the requisite originality to be protectable. In contrast, the text listing the contents of the package is probably not protectable expression. Statements of fact, such as packaging contents are likely not protectable.

Alternatively, there is an argument that the location/arrangement of the text on Tableware's box in combination with the overhead photograph may be copyrightable even if the text itself is unprotectable. Because the overhead photograph and arrangement of text for both boxes are almost identical, it is likely that Tableware will be able to show that Casual's box design is substantially similar to Tableware's. Thus, Tableware has a strong argument that Casual copied Tableware's copyrighted box design without authorization.

POINTS TO REMEMBER

- Today, a copyright in a work published in the U.S. will expire after the life of the author plus 70 years. If the author is anonymous, pseudonymous, or the work is a work made for hire, the copyright term lasts 95 years from the date of publication or 120 years from creation, whichever is less.

- If a work is "made for hire" then the law considers the employer or person that the work was made for the author of the work.

- A copyright owner has the right to reproduce, distribute, perform or display her work, create derivative works, and prevent unauthorized copying of her work.

- To prevail in a copyright infringement suit, the plaintiff must show that she owns a valid copyright in the work and that the defendant made an unauthorized copy of the protected expression contained in the work.

- The sale of a product that may be used to make infringing copies of a work does not constitute contributory infringement if the product in question has legitimate and unobjectionable purposes.

CHAPTER 9

Copyright Infringement: Defenses and Remedies

This Chapter summarizes defenses to copyright infringement and the available remedies for copyright infringement. Technology has made it easier to share and infringe copyrighted work. In response, the law has evolved to balance the rights of copyright holders with the interest of media consumers. For example, the Digital Millennium Copyright Act ("DMCA"), outlines rules for online service providers and their treatment of copyrighted material. This chapter will guide the student through the test for fair use and provide a checklist to assist the student in working through copyright infringement defenses and remedies. In addition, this Chapter summarizes the exceptions for Online Service Providers in the DMCA.

COPYRIGHT INFRINGEMENT: DEFENSES AND REMEDIES REVIEW

Defenses and Safe Harbors

There are several defenses to copyright infringement. At a minimum, IP survey students should be familiar with the fair use defense. In addition, the Digital Millennium Copyright Act created "safe harbors" to shield specific companies from copyright infringement lawsuits. This section summarizes the fair use defense, the DMCA safe harbors, and other defenses to copyright infringement that are most commonly covered in an IP survey course.

Fair Use

Fair use is an affirmative defense to copyright infringement. The defense is set forth in 17 U.S.C. § 107. The preamble of the statute states that the fair use of a copyrighted work is not infringement and lists several purposes that may qualify as a fair use: "criticism, comment, news reporting, teaching (including multiple copies for classroom use), scholarship, or research."[1] Students should remember that the purposes listed are just examples and are not intended to be comprehensive. The main part of the statute, lists four factors to be considered when determining whether a use of a work is a fair use: (1) the purpose and character of the use; (2) the nature of the copyrighted work; (3) the amount and substantiality of the portion used in relation to the copyrighted work as a whole; and (4) the effect of the use upon the potential market for the value of the copyrighted work.

The statute omits any guidance on how to weigh each factor or how to balance the four factors. Factors are not considered in isolation. Thus, courts use their discretion to evaluate each factor and upon a consideration of all the evidence, courts make a fair use determination. Each factor will be discussed in turn below.

Purpose and Character of the Use

The first fair use factor focuses on the purpose and character of the use of the copyrighted work. The preamble of § 107 lists several purposes that will likely be a fair use: criticism, comment, news reporting, teaching, scholarship, or research. Use can be characterized in numerous ways such as educational or commercial. The use of a work for non-commercial purposes such as recording a television program so you can watch it at your leisure (time-shifting) is a fair use.[2] While the commercial use of a work cuts against a finding of fair use, the rule is not absolute.

A court may also look at an alleged infringer's motivations to use the copyrighted work. Using a work in bad faith may weigh against a finding of fair use.[3] In contrast, making copies of computer code for the purposes of reverse engineering the code to study and understand elements of the software that are not eligible for copyright protection is a fair use.[4]

In some cases, the purpose and character of the use is transformative. A determination that a use is transformative weighs in favor of a finding of fair use. A work is transformative if the material taken from the original work has been changed by the addition of new expression, meaning, information, aesthetics, insights or understanding. A parody is an example of a potentially

---

[1] 17 U.S.C. § 107 (2017).

[2] *See e.g.,* Sony Corp. of Am. v. Universal City Studios, Inc., 464 U.S. 417, 454–455 (1984), *superseded by statute,* Digital Millenium Copyright Act of 1998, Pub. L. No. 115–64.

[3] Harper & Row, Publrs. v. Nation Enters., 471 U.S. 539, 562 (1985).

[4] *See e.g.,* Sega Enters. v. Accolade, Inc., 977 F.2d 1510 (9th Cir. 1992).

transformative work.[5] A parody is the imitation and distortion of an existing work for various purposes such as criticism. In addition, Google's copying of entire books in order to make them searchable using its Google Books product has been held to be a transformative use.[6] In contrast, in *Am. Geophysical Union v. Texaco Inc.*, the court found that the mechanical photocopying of scientific articles was not transformative and therefore weighed against a finding of fair use.[7]

The Nature of the Copyrighted Work

The second fair use factor focuses on the copyrighted work itself—what is it and how much protection is it afforded under copyright law? This factor is based on the recognition that some works are closer to the core of intended copyright protection than others.[8] Under the second factor, creative works are offered more protection than factual works. For example, the use of a fictional story is more likely to weigh against a finding of fair use, whereas the use of a less creative, scientific article may weigh in favor of a finding of fair use.[9]

The Amount and Substantiality of the Portion Used in Relation to the Copyrighted Work as a Whole

The third fair use factor analyzes the amount and substantiality of the use of the copyrighted work. The third factor is concerned with the amount of the copyrighted work that was used as well as the characteristics of the subject matter that was taken. A finding that only a small amount of the copyrighted work was used in relation to the whole would weigh in favor of fair use. Alternatively, if the accused infringer used a large amount of the copyrighted work it would likely weigh against a finding of fair use. The third factor also analyzes the substance of what was used. For example, in *Harper & Row, Publrs. v. Nation Enters.*, the Supreme Court found that the use of 300 words in a 20,000-word manuscript weighed against a finding of fair use because the 300 words taken could be considered the most substantive part of the manuscript.[10]

A determination of the third factor may be affected by the purpose and character of the alleged infringing use. For example, a use in which the defendant makes an exact copy of the copyrighted work may be interpreted differently based on why the copy was made

---

[5] Campbell v. Acuff-Rose Music, Inc., 510 U.S. 569, 579 (1994).

[6] *See* Authors Guild, Inc. v. Google Inc., 954 F. Supp. 2d 282 (S.D.N.Y. 2013).

[7] Am. Geophysical Union v. Texaco Inc., 60 F.3d 913, 923 (2d Cir. 1994).

[8] 4 Nimmer on Copyright § 13.05 (2017).

[9] Am. Geophysical Union v. Texaco Inc., 60 F.3d 913, 925 (2d Cir. 1994).

[10] Harper & Row, Publrs. v. Nation Enters., 471 U.S. 539, 599 (1985).

and how it is used by the defendant. Making a copy of a scientific article in its entirety for the purpose of future retrieval and reference weighs against a finding of fair use.[11] In contrast, if the use is a parody, then enough of the copyrighted work must be taken for the parody to conjure up the original.[12] Similarly, in *Bill Graham Archives v. Dorling Kindersley Ltd.*, the amount and substantiality factor weighed in favor of fair use when the defendant copied the entirety of the plaintiff's historical poster images and reduced them in size so that the posters could be printed into a book.[13]

The Effect of the Use upon the Potential Market for the Value of the Copyrighted Work

The fourth fair use factor examines the effect of the alleged infringing use on the commercial market for the copyrighted work. A use that supplants demand for the copyrighted work weighs against a finding of fair use. In contrast, a determination that the alleged infringing use is not a commercial substitute for the original work or a derivative of the original work weighs in favor of fair use. In applying this factor, courts ignore the adverse impact that a critique of the copyrighted work has on its market.[14] In addition, if the use is transformative, courts are less likely to find that the use supplants demand for the copyrighted work.[15]

DMCA Safe Harbors

Modern technology makes it easy for parties to conduct activity that might be copyright infringement. In turn, copyright law has responded to technological advancement in several ways: imposing limit controls on technology used for copying; establishing a performance right for digital transmissions; criminalizing acts such as using a recording device in a movie theater; making it unlawful to circumvent technological protection measures that control access to the work; and providing a mechanism for online service providers ("OSPs") to protect themselves against claims of copyright infringement.

During the Internet's infancy, many OSPs were concerned about their exposure to liability based on the potentially infringing acts of

---

[11] *See e.g.,* Am. Geophysical Union v. Texaco Inc., 60 F.3d 913 (2d Cir. 1994).

[12] Campbell v. Acuff-Rose Music, Inc., 510 U.S. 569, 588 (1994).

[13] Bill Graham Archives v. Dorling Kindersley Ltd., 448 F.3d 605, 613 (2d Cir. 2006) (finding that the use was transformative and outweighed the fact that the defendant copied the plaintiff's entire image).

[14] 4 Nimmer on Copyright § 13.05 (2017).

[15] Campbell v. Acuff-Rose Music, Inc., 510 U.S. 569, 591 (1994) ("But when, on the contrary, the second use is transformative, market substitution is at least less certain, and market harm may not be so readily inferred.")

their customers. In response, as part of the DMCA, Congress implemented safe harbor provisions to protect OSPs. If an OSP qualifies for protection under the safe harbor provision, then it is not liable for remedies typically available in a copyright infringement suit.[16] The safe harbor provisions are set forth in 17 U.S.C. § 512.

Eligibility

To be eligible for protection under a safe harbor, an entity must: (1) be a service provider; (2) adopt, implement and, inform subscribers of a termination policy for repeat infringers; (3) accommodate and not interfere with standard technical measures used by copyright owners to identify and protect copyrighted works and (4) satisfy the specific requirements for one of the activities set forth in the statute.[17]

Activities

Generally, there are four eligible activities in § 512 that students should be aware of: (a) transistor digital network communications, (b) system caching, (c) information residing on systems or networks at direction of users, and (d) information location tools. In addition to the general eligibility requirements, the statute specifies additional conditions that must be met for each activity. For details on these conditions, students should refer to the specific statutory language as necessary. The eligible activities are summarized below.

Transistor Digital Network Communications

Section 512(a) defines transistor digital network communications as "transmitting, routing, or providing connections for, material through a system or network controlled or operated by or for the service provider, or by reason of the intermediate and transient storage of that material in the course of such transmitting, routing, or providing connections."

System Caching

Section 512(b) defines system caching as "the intermediate and temporary storage of material on a system or network controlled or operated by or for the service provider."

---

[16] The limitations on remedies is subject to an exception set forth in 17 U.S.C. § 512(j) (2017).

[17] 17 U.S.C. § 512(i) (2017).

Information Residing on Systems or Networks at Direction of Users

Section 512(c) defines information residing on systems or networks at direction of users as "the storage at the direction of a user of material that resides on a system or network controlled or operated by or for the service provider."

Information Location Tools

Section 512 (d) defines information location tools as "the provider referring or linking users to an online location containing infringing material or infringing activity, by using information location tools, including a directory, index, reference, pointer, or hypertext link."

Other Defenses

This section summarizes other defenses to copyright infringement that are generally covered in an IP survey course.

Independent Creation

Evidence that the defendant created a work independently is a defense to copyright infringement.

Consent/License

In defense to a copyright infringement suit, a defendant may assert that he obtained the copyright owner's consent or a license to use the copyrighted work.

Inequitable Conduct

The inequitable conduct defense may be available to a defendant if there is evidence that the copyright owner obtained the copyright by fraud or misleading the Copyright Office.

Copyright Misuse

As a defense, a defendant may argue that a copyright owner is asserting broader rights than the copyright statute provides. Copyright misuse is intended to prevent copyright owners from abusing their rights to gain an advantage over their competitors.

Statute of Limitations

Under § 507, the statute of limitations for civil actions is three years and five years for criminal actions.[18]

---

[18] 17 U.S.C. § 507 (2017).

Remedies

This section summarizes the basic remedies available for copyright infringement. Copyright law provides for the recovery of damages as well as injunctive relief.

Injunctions

Section 502(a) authorizes a court to grant preliminary and permanent injunctions to prevent or restrain copyright infringement.[19] A court may also impound and destroy infringing copies under § 503. In determining whether to award injunctive relief, courts use an equitable framework in lieu of automatically granting an injunction.[20]

Damages

Actual Damages and Profits

Section 504 states that a copyright infringer is liable for the copyright owner's damages suffered as a result of the infringement and the infringer's profits that are attributable to the infringement.[21]

Statutory Damages

As an alternative to actual damages, a plaintiff may recover statutory damages. Congress provided for statutory damages in part because determining actual damages and profits in a copyright infringement case is difficult. A copyright owner may decide to recover statutory damages at any time before final judgement. Statutory damages are available to owners of registered works in the amount of $700 to $30,000 per infringed work.[22] If the copyright owner proves her work was willfully infringed, the damage amount may increase to $150,000. Conversely, if the infringer was unaware of the infringement, courts have the discretion to lower the damage award to as little as $200 per infringed work.

Attorney Fees

Finally, § 505 states that the court, at its discretion, may award attorney fees to the prevailing parties.[23] In determining whether to award attorney fees, courts consider a number of factors related to the litigation posture and conduct of the parties including, but not limited to frivolousness, motivation, and litigation misconduct.

---

[19] 17 U.S.C. § 502(a).

[20] eBay Inc. v. MercExchange, LLC, 547 U.S. 388, 391–392 (2006).

[21] 17 U.S.C. § 504.

[22] 17 U.S.C. § 504(c).

[23] 17 U.S.C. § 505.

COPYRIGHT INFRINGEMENT:
DEFENSES AND REMEDIES
CHECKLIST

With the above Review in mind, the Copyright Infringement: Defenses and Remedies Checklist is presented below.

A. **FAIR USE.** Determine whether the defendant made a fair use of the plaintiff's work. Fair use of a copyrighted work is not copyright infringement. Whether a use is a fair use is based on the consideration of four factors.

1. **Purpose and Character of the Use.** Consider the alleged infringing use and evaluate its purpose and character. The use of a copyrighted work for the purposes of criticism, comment, news reporting, teaching, scholarship, or research are more likely to weigh in favor of fair use. A determination that the use is transformative (changed by the addition of new expression, meaning, information, aesthetics, insights or understanding) also weighs in favor of a fair use determination.

2. **The Nature of the Copyrighted Work.** What is the allegedly infringed work? The law recognizes stronger copyright protection in creative works than it does in more factual works. The less creative the work, the more likely this factor will weigh in favor of a finding of fair use.

3. **The Amount and Substantiality of the Portion Used in Relation to the Copyrighted Work as a Whole.** How much of the alleged infringed work was used? The less the amount of the copyrighted work used, the more likely this factor weighs in favor of fair use. Also, consider the substance of what was copied from the alleged infringed work? If only a small amount of the copyrighted work is used, this factor may still weigh against a finding of fair use if the defendant took the most substantive portion of the copyrighted work.

4. **The Effect of the Use upon the Potential Market for the Value of the Copyrighted Work.** What is the effect of the alleged infringing use on the market for the copyrighted work? If the alleged infringing use will supplant the copyrighted work in the marketplace then this factor weighs against a finding of fair use.

B. **ONLINE SERVICE PROVIDER SAFE HARBORS.** The DMCA includes safe harbor provisions to protect OSPs (with certain exceptions) from copyright infringement liability. To take advantage of the safe harbor provisions an entity must meet the general eligibility requirements and participate in an eligible service activity.

1. **Eligibility.** Does the entity satisfy the general eligibility requirements for the OSP safe harbor provisions?

   a. **OSP.** An entity must be an online service provider.

   b. **Termination Policy.** An entity must adopt, implement and, inform subscribers of a termination policy for repeat infringers.

   c. **Technical Measures.** An entity must accommodate and not interfere with standard technical measures used by copyright owners to identify and protect copyrighted works.

   d. **Activities.** An entity must satisfy the specific requirements for one of the activities set forth in 17 U.S.C. § 512.

2. **Activities.** Determine whether the activities of the OSP satisfy the eligibility requirements set forth in the statute. An OSP that participates in one of the activities set forth in 17 U.S.C. § 512 may be eligible for the safe harbor provisions.

   a. **Transistor Digital Network Communications.** Section 512(a) defines this activity as "transmitting, routing, or providing connections for, material through a system or network controlled or operated by or for the service provider, or by reason of the intermediate and transient storage of that material in the course of such transmitting, routing, or providing connections."

   b. **System Caching.** Section 512(b) defines this activity as "the intermediate and temporary storage of material on a system or network controlled or operated by or for the service provider."

   c. **Information Residing on Systems or Networks at Direction of Users.** Section 512(c) defines this activity as "the storage at the direction of a user of material that resides on a system or network controlled or operated by or for the service provider."

   d. **Information Location Tools.** Section 512(d) defines this activity as "the provider referring or linking users to an online location containing infringing material or infringing activity, by using information location tools, including a directory, index, reference, pointer, or hypertext link."

C. **OTHER DEFENSES.** Determine whether other defenses to copyright infringement are applicable.

1. **Independent Creation.** Did the defendant create the alleged infringing work independently? If so, independent creation is a defense to copyright infringement.

2. **Consent or License.** Does the defendant have the copyright owner's consent or a license to use the copyrighted work? Evidence of consent or a license may be defense to copyright infringement.

3. **Inequitable Conduct.** If there is evidence that the copyright owner obtained his copyright by fraud, or misled the Copyright Office then the defendant may be successful at asserting the inequitable conduct defense.

4. **Copyright Misuse.** As a defense, a defendant may argue that a copyright owner is asserting broader rights than the copyright statute provides.

5. **Statute of Limitations.** Has the statute of limitations run for a cause of action under the copyright statute? The statute of limitations for civil actions is three years and five years for criminal actions.

D. **REMEDIES.** Determine what remedies are available to the plaintiff. Copyright law provides for both damages and injunctive relief.

1. **Injunctions.** Based on established principles of equity, a court may order a preliminary and permanent injunction. In some instances, a court may impound or order the destruction of infringing copies.

2. **Damages.** In a copyright infringement suit, a court may award several different types of damages.

   a. **Actual Damages and Profits.** A plaintiff may recover damages that were suffered as a direct result of the defendant's infringement. A plaintiff may also obtain damages based on the defendant's profits that were directly attributable to the copyright infringement.

   b. **Statutory Damages.** In the alternative to calculating damages and defendant's profits, the copyright statute sets forth statutory damages for copyright infringement. Statutory damages are available in the amount of $700 to $30,000 per infringed work. If the work was willfully infringed, the damage amount may increase to $150,000. If the infringer was unaware of the infringement, the damage award may be as little as $200 per infringed work.

c.   **Attorney Fees.** Courts may award attorney fees to the prevailing parties based on the litigation posture and conduct of the parties.

ILLUSTRATIVE PROBLEMS

Here are two problems that illustrate how the Checklist can be used to resolve copyright infringement questions.

■ PROBLEM 9.1 ■

Ben Jenkins is a photojournalist. On July 4, 2015, Jenkins was assigned to cover a local camping festival at a nearby national park. Jenkins took a photograph of some boys raising the American flag on a small hill above their campground. Jenkins named the photo "Flag Boys."

The photo was published in The Plainview, a local paper, the next day. Later that year, The Plainview's general counsel filed for and obtained a Certificate of Registration for the photo from the U.S. Copyright Office. In 2016, from January to June, The Plainview earned substantial revenue by licensing "Flag Boys" to other media companies.

Grady Huff hosts a nationally televised show called the Huff Report on the Patriot News Network. Huff maintains a website that is associated with the show. On July 4, 2016, to advertise his show commemorating Independence Day, Huff found an image of Flag Boys using an Internet search and posted the image on the Huff Report website.

Huff edited the image in two ways. First, he added the text "#July4" to the lower left corner of the image. Second, Huff cropped the image to focus more on the boys and remove some of the empty sky in the background. On his show that aired July 4, 2016, Huff did not discuss or mention the "Flag Boys" photograph.

The Plainview learned of Huff's use of the photograph on July 10, 2016. The Plainview requested that Huff remove "Flag Boys" from his website. Huff refused.

In the ensuing litigation for copyright infringement, discuss Huff's potential fair use defense.

Analysis

A copyright confers exclusive rights on the author or owner of the copyrighted work. However, the doctrine of fair use places limits on these exclusive rights. Specifically, 17 U.S.C. § 107 states that the fair use of a copyrighted work is not infringement. The four factors to be considered when determining whether a use of a work is a fair use are (1) the purpose and character of the use; (2) the nature of the copyrighted work; (3) the amount and substantiality of the portion used in relation to the copyrighted work as a whole; and (4) the effect of the use upon the potential market for the value of the copyrighted work. In making a determination, courts weigh all the factors.

The Purpose and Character of the Use

The first factor examines why and how the copyrighted work was used by the defendant and also evaluates whether the defendant's use was transformative. A use is transformative if it adds to the original work in a way that creates something new and different.

Here, it is likely that the first factor weighs against a finding of fair use. Huff's purpose for using "Flag Boys" was to advertise his show. A court could find advertising to be a commercial use. Further, while Huff hosts a news show, the facts indicate that "Flag Boys" or the festival were not discussed on the television show. Thus, Huff's posting of "Flag Boys" without more is unlikely to qualify as criticism, comment, or news reporting. Further, Huff's modification of "Flag Boys" is not transformative. Huff simply added a hashtag to the bottom of the photo and cropped it to eliminate some background from the photograph. The work is barely altered and can be immediately identified as the "Flag Boys" photograph. Further, Huff's alterations fail to add new meaning or insight.

The Nature of the Copyrighted Work

The second factor focuses on the copyrighted work. The law recognizes that creative works are closer to the core of copyright protection than more factual based works. Here, the second factor will likely weigh in favor of a finding of fair use. "Flag Boys" is a photograph of a non-fictional event in a public setting. Jenkins did not ask the boys to pose for a photo nor did he stage or design the scene. "Flag Boys" is a photo captured for news gathering and is an example of photojournalism. Where similar photos were at issue, courts have held that the second factor weighed in favor of fair use.

The Amount and Substantiality of the Portion Used in Relation to the Copyrighted Work as a Whole

This factor examines the quantity and substance of the work used. If the defendant used more of the copyrighted work than necessary, this factor weighs against a finding of fair use. This factor is influenced by the first two factors. For some purposes, it may be necessary to use the whole work. Further, it may be necessary to use almost all of a photograph to maintain its meaning to a viewer.

In similar cases involving photographs like "Flag Boys" courts have found this factor to be neutral. Huff cropped the original photograph while at the same time maintaining the image of the boys raising the flag. Further, copying less of the photo would not serve the tangential purpose of commemorating July 4th. Thus, a court will likely conclude that the third factor does not favor either party.

The Effect of the Use upon the Potential Market for the Value of the Copyrighted Work

The last factor examines whether the defendant's use usurps the market of the original work. In assessing this factor, a court may consider how transformative the use is and the impact of the use on the plaintiff's potential licensing royalties.

Here, this factor weighs against a finding of fair use. As stated above, Huff's use of "Flag Boys" is not transformative. Thus, it is more likely to supplant demand for the "Flag Boys" photograph. The facts further indicate that The Plainview earns substantial licensing royalties on "Flag Boys." In sum, Huff's behavior signals that there is a danger that other organizations will use "Flag Boys" without paying the licensing fee.

Summary

Considering the analysis as a whole, it is likely that Huff did not make a fair use of "Flag Boys." The first and fourth factors weigh against a finding of fair use. The second factor weighs in favor of fair use but is generally less determinative than the other factors. Finally, the third factor is neutral. Thus, Huff's fair use defense is likely to fail.

■ PROBLEM 9.2 ■

Photostop, Inc. ("Photostop") operates a website called Photostop.com. The website allows users to upload photographs to the Internet for others to view. All the content on Photostop.com is user generated. Photostop itself does not contribute any content to the website. Photostop offers its website services to its users for free and uses advertising as its primary source of revenue.

Photostop's Terms of Use prohibits users from uploading material that infringes another's copyright. The Terms of Use also specifies that Photostop has the power to terminate a user account for any repeat violations of any of its Terms of Use.

The main page of the Photostop website includes a link to a "take-down notice procedure." The information on this page provides instructions on how to notify a designated agent of potential copyright infringement. If Photostop receives a take-down notice, it removes the infringing images and informs the copyright holder that the content has been removed. Photostop also notifies the user who posted the allegedly infringing image. The user is given an opportunity to respond to the take-down notice through the Photostop website.

George Willow is an artist. Willow specializes in taking photographs of domesticated animals in costumes. Willow has an online store which is the exclusive licensor of his photographs. All of Willow's work is registered with the U.S. Copyright Office. Willow uses watermark technology to identify unlicensed copies of his images.

Willow discovered several of his photographs displayed by users on the Photostop website without his authorization. All of Willow's photographs on the Photostop website had a large "W" watermark in the bottom right corner. Willow sent Photostop take-down notices concerning his photographs. The next day, Photostop removed the photos from users' accounts on the Photostop website.

Does Photostop meet the threshold requirements to qualify for the DMCA's safe harbor provisions?

Analysis

This question tests your basic understanding of the threshold requirements for the DMCA safe harbor provisions.[24] In order to qualify for the safe harbor provisions (1) a party must be a service provider, (2) must have a policy for terminating the accounts of repeat infringers, and (3) must not interfere with standard technical measures used by copyright owners to identify or protect copyrighted works.

Service Provider

A service provider as defined in the statute includes a large number of entities. An entity that provides online services to a user

---

[24] Note that once the threshold requirements are met, a complete analysis of safe harbor eligibility would include an analysis involving the four eligible activities under § 512.

including the transmission of material of the user's choosing is a service provider. Here, the Photostop website allows users to upload and share images with other users. Youtube.com, a video hosting site, provides a similar service for videos and qualifies as a service provider under the DMCA. By analogy, Photostop would also qualify as a service provider under the DMCA.

Policy for Termination of Users

To qualify for the safe harbor provisions, a service provider must "1) adopt a policy that provides for the termination of service access for repeat copyright infringers in appropriate circumstances; 2) inform users of the service policy; and 3) implement the policy in a reasonable manner."[25]

The facts indicate that Photostop may meet the second threshold requirement. Photostop has a policy published on its website that allows copyright holders to identify and request infringing material be removed. Further, Photstop's policy indicates that repeat infringers' accounts can be terminated. Finally, Photostop responded to Willow's takedown request in less than 24 hours. Photostop's policies and actions seem to meet all the requirements specified above.

Technical Measures

Photostop meets the third threshold requirement if it accommodates and does not interfere with standard technical measures used by copyright holders to identify their work. Here, the facts state that Willow uses watermarks to identify unlicensed copies of his images. All of the images Willow discovered on the Photostop website had a "W" watermark. Presumably, Willow was able to easily identify his images because of the watermark. It appears that the Photostop website accommodates the use of watermarks and there is no evidence that Photostop prevents the use of watermarks. Thus, there is a strong argument that Photostop meets the third threshold requirement.

Conclusion

In sum, it is likely that Photostop meets the threshold requirements to qualify for the DMCA's safe harbor provisions.

POINTS TO REMEMBER

- The four factors to be considered in determining whether a defendant has made fair use of a copyrighted work are: (1) the

---

[25] Corbis Corp. v. Amazon.com, Inc., 351 F. Supp. 2d 1090, 1100 (W.D. Wash. 2004).

purpose and character of the use; (2) the nature of the copyrighted work; (3) the amount and substantiality of the portion used in relation to the copyrighted work as a whole; and (4) the effect of the use upon the potential market for the value of the copyrighted work.

• Courts do not evaluate the four fair use factors in isolation. One factor may influence one or more of the other factors.

• A work is transformative if the material taken from the original work has been changed by the addition of new expression, meaning, information, aesthetics, insights or understanding.

• In order to qualify for the DMCA safe harbor provisions, a party must be a service provider, must have a policy for terminating the accounts of repeat infringers, and must not interfere with standard technical measures used by copyright owners to identify or protect copyrighted works.

• The copyright statute provides for statutory damages as an alternative to actual damages and profits.

CHAPTER 10

Trade Secrets

This book concludes with a chapter on trade secret law. Like trademark, copyright, and patent law, trade secret law is a robust topic. Most IP survey courses focus on two questions. How are rights in trade secrets acquired and how does a trade secret owner enforce those rights?

To answer these questions, you will study a combination of state and federal law. Despite differences across jurisdictions, there are some universal themes. First, almost anything can be eligible for trade secret protection. Second, misappropriation occurs when a party unlawfully acquires a trade secret.

A large percentage of trade secret misappropriation cases arise in the context of departing employees. The law attempts to balance employee mobility with employers' rights. This chapter will summarize the law on trade secret subject matter and misappropriation in a way that will allow you to systematically identify the issues and apply the correct legal rules to most exam questions.

TRADE SECRETS REVIEW

Defining a Trade Secret

State and federal statutes vary in how they define a trade secret. In general, the definition is not limited to a particular category of subject matter.[1] A broad, working definition of a trade secret is (1) any information, device, method, formula, technique or process that (2) derives independent economic value from (3) not being generally known or readily ascertainable by others (that can obtain economic value from its disclosure or use) and (4) is the subject of reasonable efforts to maintain its secrecy. Each one of these elements is discussed in detail below.

---

[1] 1–1 Milgrim on Trade Secrets § 1.01 (2017).

Subject Matter

Almost anything can be eligible for trade secret protection. Any formula, process, technique, pattern, compilation, program, plan, design, software, machine, customer list, or business information could be trade secret subject matter. Modifications or improvements to existing processes or products may also be eligible for trade secret protection.[2] Generally, trade secret subject matter concerns business operations or a product, and is used by a party over a sustained period of time.[3]

Economic Value

Almost anything that has economic value maybe eligible for trade secret protection. If subject matter is competitively significant, it will likely have economic value.[4] For example, in *Metallurgical Indus. v. Fourtek, Inc.*, modifications made to furnaces for carbide reclamation were eligible for trade secret protection in part because they gave the owner a commercial advantage over its competitors.[5]

Parties may also protect business information as trade secrets to gain a commercial advantage. "Blind alleys" are an example of information eligible for trade secret protection. Blind alleys are unproductive actions or information. In some industries, knowing what does not work can be as valuable as knowing what does. Knowledge of blind alleys allows parties to be more efficient with their resources. Other examples of subject matter that may be eligible for trade secret protection because of the commercial advantage they bestow on the owner include market research, customer lists, and business plans.

Secrecy

Secrecy is an essential element of a trade secret. A trade secret cannot be public knowledge. In addition, a trade secret owner must attempt to keep trade secret subject matter a secret.

Not Generally Known or Readily Ascertainable

Subject matter may not be eligible for trade secret protection if it is generally known. Also, if the information is known in a particular industry then it is not a secret. However, the requirement that a trade secret not be generally known is different from the statutory requirements in patent law. The law does not require trade secret

---

[2] Metallurgical Indus. v. Fourtek, Inc., 790 F.2d 1195, 1202 (5th Cir. 1986).

[3] 1–1 Milgrim on Trade Secrets § 1.01 (2017).

[4] *See* UTSA § 7 Commissioner's Comment.

[5] Metallurgical Indus. v. Fourtek, Inc., 790 F.2d 1195, 1201 (5th Cir. 1986).

subject matter to be novel or non-obvious. Thus, a simple improvement or repair on an existing device could be eligible for trade secret protection.

If a third party can learn of another's trade secret through proper means, then the trade secret may be considered readily ascertainable and therefore ineligible for trade secret protection. For example, trade secret information published in a patent is readily ascertainable and therefore not eligible for protection.[6] Similarly, if a trade secret owner publishes customer information on its website, that information is readily ascertainable and no longer considered a secret.[7]

Maintenance of Secrecy

Subject matter eligible for trade secret protection must be subject to reasonable efforts to maintain its secrecy. Examples of secrecy efforts include physical security measures, non-disclosure agreements (NDAs), digital security measures, and implementing internal procedures for handling sensitive information. Restricting building visitors to certain areas or keeping certain documents locked in a vault are concrete examples of security measures that may be used to protect trade secrets.[8]

The maintenance of secrecy requirement has an evidentiary purpose. The presence of efforts to maintain secrecy is evidence that the subject matter at issue has value. Also, it may evidence that the defendant circumvented secrecy measures to acquire access to the trade secret.

Whether the secrecy measure employed is reasonable depends on a number of factors. These factors include characteristics of the party purporting to own the trade secret (industry type, size, employee profile) and the nature of the trade secret itself.

Disclosure of Trade Secrets

Generally, subject matter is eligible for trade secret protection until it is disclosed and no longer a secret. Thus, an unprotected disclosure of a trade secret will likely forfeit any prospective protection under trade secret law.[9]

Voluntary disclosures by the trade secret owner are examples of unprotected disclosures. Therefore, a trade secret owner that

---

[6] 1–1 Milgrim on Trade Secrets § 1.03 (2017).

[7] Sky Capital Grp., Ltd. Liab. Co. v. Rojas, 2009 WL 1370938, at *4 (D. Idaho 2009).

[8] 1–1 Milgrim on Trade Secrets § 1.04 (2017).

[9] Id. at § 1.05 (2017).

discloses their trade secret in a publicly available academic journal will likely jeopardize their trade secret protection in that information. Similarly, secrecy is lost if the trade secret is disclosed in a patent publication.

In some instances, trade secrets may also be lawfully disclosed by third parties. For example, a third party that independently discovers and publishes a trade secret defeats everyone's rights to trade secret protection in the published information. In contrast, a third party's unauthorized disclosures of a trade secret are unlikely to jeopardize the secrecy status of the disclosed subject matter.[10]

A trade secret may be embodied in a physical product that is sold in commerce. If another can discover the trade secret by inspection of a marketed product then the secret nature of the subject matter is lost.[11] Marketing activity can include a sale, but could come in the form of advertising, white papers, informational websites, etc. In sum, trade secret subject matter embodied in a product may become public knowledge once that product is offered for sale.

The law does not require a trade secret owner to maintain her trade secret in complete secrecy.[12] The trade secret owner may need to disclose the trade secret to her employees so that they can use it to do their job. In some instances, she may need to disclose trade secret subject matter to a third party that agrees to keep it a secret.[13] Limited disclosures may not negatively impact the disclosed subject matter's eligibility for trade secret protection.[14] This may be accomplished by a contractual agreement such as a Non-Disclosure Agreement (NDA).

Misappropriation of Trade Secrets

This section summarizes trade secret misappropriation. A cause of action for the misappropriation of a trade secret requires (1) that the subject matter at issue qualify as a trade secret and be treated as such, and (2) that the subject matter be acquired, used or disclosed in a wrongful act.

Improper Means

A party may be liable for trade secret misappropriation if it obtains or discloses another's trade secret by improper means. A means is improper if it falls below the standards of commercial

---

[10] Id. at § 1.03 (2017).

[11] Id. at § 1.05 (2017).

[12] Id. at § 1.01 (2017).

[13] Id. at § 1.04 (2017).

[14] *See* Data General Corp. v. Digital Computer Controls, Inc., 297 A.2d 433 (Del. Ct. Ch. 1971), *aff'd* 297 A.2d 437 (Del. S. Ct. 1971).

morality and reasonable conduct.[15] For example, in *E.I. Du Pont deNemours & Co. v. Christopher*, the court found that the defendant's actions of taking aerial photographs of the plaintiff's facility while it was under construction was unreasonable and thus an improper means of obtaining trade secret information about the plaintiff's process for producing methanol.[16] Improper means may also include the commission of a criminal act such as theft, fraud, bribery or various forms of espionage.

Breach of Confidence

A party may also be liable for trade secret misappropriation if it discloses another's trade secret by breaching an express or implied confidential relationship. An express confidential relationship exists if a party makes an express promise of confidentiality prior to the disclosure of the trade secret.[17] An implied confidential relationship exists between parties if a trade secret was disclosed to a party and that party knew or had reason to know that the disclosure was intended to be in confidence and the other party to the disclosure was reasonable in inferring that the person consented to an obligation of confidentiality.[18] An implied confidential relationship may arise between parties that share trade secret information as a part of a larger business transaction.[19] In contrast, a party that sends unsolicited trade secret information to another party, likely has not created a confidential relationship.

Indirect Liability

A party may also be liable for misappropriation of trade secrets if they receive and use trade secret information that they know was obtained improperly from the trade secret owner.[20] A scenario that raises this issue usually involves an employee that has left one company (Company A) to work for a competitor (Company B). In this scenario, if Company B knowingly obtains trade secrets owned by Company A because the employee breached an express or implied duty, then Company B could also be liable for trade secret misappropriation.

---

[15] Restatement of Torts § 757, comment f at 10 (1939).

[16] *See* E. I. du Pont deNemours & Co. v. Christopher, 431 F.2d 1012 (5th Cir. 1970), *cert. denied*, 400 U.S. 1024 (1971).

[17] Restatement 3rd Unfair Competition § 41 (a).

[18] Restatement 3rd Unfair Competition § 41 (b).

[19] *See, e.g.,* Smith v. Dravo Corp., 203 F.2d 369 (7th Cir. 1953).

[20] 2–7 Milgrim on Trade Secrets § 7.02 (2017).

Defenses to Trade Secret Misappropriation

Trade secret law deters the acquisition of trade secrets using improper means. A party that acquires a trade secret by proper means is not liable for misappropriation. Thus, as a defense to trade secret misappropriation, a defendant may argue that he used proper means to obtain the trade secret.

Proper means for obtaining a trade secret include (1) independent discovery, (2) from public observation or published literature, (3) discovery under a license from the trade secret owner, and reverse engineering.[21] Reverse engineering is "starting with the known product and working backward to divine the process which aided in its development or manufacture."[22] However, obtaining a trade secret through reverse engineering is not proper where the means used to get the information necessary to reverse engineer is not in the public domain.[23]

Remedies for Trade Secret Misappropriation

A plaintiff may obtain damages or injunctive relief as a remedy for trade secret misappropriation. Both remedies are summarized below.

Damages

A plaintiff may obtain damages as a remedy for past harm caused by trade secret misappropriation. In order to obtain damages, the plaintiff must show that the misappropriated trade secret was used by the defendant to the economic detriment of the trade secret owner. If successful, the plaintiff may obtain an award in the amount of its lost profits, the defendant's profits, or some combination of the two. Finally, if the trade secret was disclosed to the public, the plaintiff may only receive damages for the period of time in which the subject matter remained a secret.

Injunctive Relief

A trade secret owner may also obtain injunctive relief. In fact, plaintiffs often seek injunctive remedies in trade secret cases.[24] A plaintiff may obtain a preliminary or permanent injunction. Both determinations depend in part on whether the plaintiff will suffer

---

[21] UTSA Comment to § 1.

[22] Kewanee v. Bircon, 416 U.S. 470, 476, 94 S. Ct. 1879, 1883 (1974).

[23] Kadant v. Seely Machine, 244 F.Supp.2d 19, 38 (N.D.N.Y. 2003) (explaining that a claim of reverse engineering does not immunize the defendant from liability for trade secret theft).

[24] 4–15 Milgrim on Trade Secrets § 15.02 (2017) ("Injunctive relief is the most commonly sought form of relief in trade secret litigation").

irreparable injury from the defendant's conduct. Permanent injunctions are terminated when the trade secret ceases to exist, e.g., is publicly disclosed.

A court can tailor injunctions based on the particular facts of a case. For example, a court may enjoin a defendant from selling a product based on misappropriated information for a limited amount of time to eliminate the defendant's commercial advantage. Generally, the period is based on the amount of time it would have taken the defendant to reverse engineer or independently discover the product.[25] Once that time period has expired, the defendant may resume selling its product.

Departing Employees

The issue of trade secret misappropriation often arises in cases where an employee leaves their current employer to pursue another opportunity. Under certain circumstances, both the departing employee and new employer could be exposed to liability for misappropriation of trade secrets. Trade secret law attempts to balance the interest of employers in protecting their trade secrets and the interest of employee mobility.

Generally, past employees are under an implied duty of confidentiality not to disclose their past employer's confidential information such as trade secrets. Employers may expressly set forth this obligation in a nondisclosure agreement. To be enforceable, nondisclosure agreements must be clear and unambiguous, exist at the time confidential information is disclosed, and must be reasonable in scope. In addition, an assignment agreement may obligate an employee to assign her employer the interest in any trade secrets she develops while she is employed with the company. The assignment agreement may also contain a trailer clause. A trailer clause obligates the employee to assign her employer the interest in any trade secrets she develops for a reasonable time period after her employment is terminated.

Departing employees are allowed to use the general knowledge and skills that they obtained during their past employment for themselves or for a new employer. Absent a non-competition agreement, departing employees may also complete with their former employer. The enforceability of noncompete agreements varies by jurisdiction. Generally, noncompete agreements must be reasonable in duration and geographic scope.

---

[25] *See e.g.,* Winston Research v. 3M, 350 F.2d 134, 141 (9th Cir. 1965) (explaining that the district court limited the duration of injunctive relief because the plaintiff's trade secrets would be disclosed to the public as a result of sales).

Finally, absent any agreements to the contrary, employers may solicit another organization's employees. However, the new employer may be liable for trade secret misappropriation if they hire an employee for the purpose of obtaining another's trade secrets.

The Defend Trade Secrets Act

Trade secret law is a combination of state and federal law. At the state level, the applicable trade secret law is generally based on the state's common law, the 1939 Restatement of Torts, and the 1979 Uniform Trade Secrets Act. At the federal level, the recently enacted Defend Trade Secrets Act ("DTSA") and the 1996 Economic Espionage Act ("EEA") form the legal framework.

The DTSA was signed into law on May 11, 2016. The DTSA amended provisions of the existing EEA. The EEA already provided for a criminal cause of action for economic espionage.[26] The DTSA creates a criminal cause of action for trade secret theft[27] and provides for a private civil cause of action for trade secret misappropriation.

In addition to these procedural changes, the DTSA includes a whistleblower provision that immunizes an individual from liability for disclosing trade secrets to the government solely for the purpose of reporting or investigating a suspected violation of law or in court documents. Further, the DTSA specifies additional remedies for trade secret misappropriation. For example, the DTSA allows for a trade secret owner to seize property to prevent the unauthorized dissemination of its trade secret.[28]

        TRADE SECRET SUBJECT MATTER
                AND MISAPPROPRIATION
                          CHECKLIST

With the above Review in mind, the Trade Secret Subject Matter and Misappropriation Checklist is presented below.

A. **DETERMINE IF THE SUBJECT MATTER IS PROTECTABLE AS A TRADE SECRET.** Determine if the subject matter at issue is eligible for trade secret protection. Whether the subject matter is protectable depends on its nature as well as how the owner treats the subject matter.

   1. **Trade Secret Subject Matter.** Unlike other areas of IP, trade secret subject matter encompasses a broad range of categories. For example, subject matter capable of being

---

[26] 18 U.S.C. § 1831.

[27] Id.

[28] Id.

protected as a trade secret includes formulas, processes, methods, techniques, machines, products, plans, designs, patterns, customer information, and business information.

2. **Economic Value.** Does the subject matter have value to its owner? Would the subject matter be of value to the owner's competitors? Would a third party pay to obtain the subject matter? If the subject matter will afford its owner or those who know it a commercial advantage, it is likely protectable as a trade secret.

3. **Not Known or Readily Ascertainable.** A trade secret must have elements of secrecy. Is the subject matter generally known to the public? Or is the subject matter generally known in the specific industry at issue? If so, it is likely not protectable as a trade secret.

4. **Maintenance of Secrecy.** Not only must trade secret subject matter be a secret, but its owner must also take reasonable steps to maintain its secrecy. Examples of reasonable steps include traditional physical measures like a safe as well as the use of confidentiality agreements. Whether the owner took reasonable steps to maintain secrecy depends on the surrounding circumstances including the nature of the trade secret subject matter.

B. **DETERMINE IF THE TRADE SECRET WAS MISAPPROPRIATED.** Assess the defendant's actions to determine whether the defendant misappropriated the trade secret.

1. **Improper Means.** How did the defendant obtain the trade secret? Did she commit a crime? Did she perform an action that is immoral or unethical? Improper means may include any action that is beneath standards of reasonable conduct.

2. **Breach of Confidence.** Examine the nature of the relationship between the defendant and trade secret owner. Did the defendant owe a duty of confidentiality (express or implied) to the owner of the trade secret? In obtaining the trade secret, did the defendant breach an express or implied duty of confidentiality? If so, the defendant has likely obtained the trade secret information improperly.

C. **CONSIDER DEFENSES TO TRADE SECRET MISAPPROPRIATION.** Consider whether the defendant obtained the trade secret by proper means.

1. **Independent Discovery.** A person that learns trade secret information through independent discovery has not used improper means to obtain the trade secret.

2. **Public Disclosure.** Learning of a trade secret by reading published literature or through public observation is not an improper method of obtaining a trade secret.

3. **Licensing.** A party that licenses a trade secret from its owner has obtained the trade secret properly. However, the issue of misappropriation may still arise if the licensee breaches a duty of confidentiality by disclosing the trade secret to a third party.

4. **Reverse Engineering.** A party may use and study a publicly available product that embodies a trade secret to learn the trade secret. This process is referred to as reverse engineering. Reverse engineering is not an improper means for obtaining a trade secret.

D. **DETERMINE THE APPROPRIATE REMEDY.** Consider the appropriate remedies for trade secret misappropriation.

1. **Damages.** If a plaintiff was harmed economically by a defendant's misappropriation of their trade secret, the plaintiff may obtain damages as a remedy. The damages award can take many forms including the plaintiff's lost profits, the defendant's profits, or some combination of the two.

2. **Injunctions.** Most plaintiffs seek injunctions to stop the defendant from using or disclosing the trade secret. Courts may tailor the injunction based on the nature of the trade secret and the facts of the case. For example, a court may enjoin a defendant from using a trade secret for a specific amount of time to restore the competitive edge the trade secret owner would have enjoyed but for the misappropriation.

ILLUSTRATIVE PROBLEMS

The following two problems illustrate how the Checklist can be used to resolve trade secret subject matter and misappropriation questions.

■ PROBLEM 10.1 ■

Skin Repair, Inc. ("Skin Repair") manufactures and sells products that aid in the healing of open wounds. Skin Repair's manufacturing system yields a product which consumers purchase because they believe that it out-performs other wound care products in the market. Skin Repair's products are made from collagen. To produce the collagen that is used in its manufacturing system, Skin Repair processes bovine cowhides to obtain a collagen mixture with a specific pH level. Bovine is known in the industry as an abundant source of collagen.

Skin Repair takes standard industry steps to prevent others from learning what it uses for raw materials, the pH level of its collagen mixture, and its manufacturing system. For example, only a select group of employees know that bovine cowhides are the raw materials for the collagen mixture. Those employees are also the only ones that know the pH level of the collagen mixture.

Legend Sciences, Inc. ("Legend"), a cosmetics manufacturer, wished to develop a wound care ointment. Scientists at legend purchased several of Skin Repair's products. After months of researching the products, Legend's scientists were able to determine that the raw materials for Skin Repair's products included bovine cowhide processed to achieve a pH level of 5. Legend published a white paper on its public website discussing the potential skin healing benefits of collagen mixtures with a pH level of 5. However, after six months of Legend's scientists failing to determine Skin Repair's manufacturing system, Legend's managers decided to cancel its efforts to develop a wound care ointment.

Skin Repair, unhappy that Legend disclosed some information about the raw materials Skin Repair uses to make its wound care products, sues Legend for trade secret misappropriation.

Is the information concerning the raw materials for Skin Repair's collagen mixture a trade secret?

Analysis

An analysis of a claim for trade secret misappropriation involves two steps. First, you must determine whether the subject matter at issue is a trade secret. Second, you must determine whether the trade secret subject matter was misappropriated. This question asks you to focus on the first step—whether the information about the raw materials is a trade secret.

A trade secret is any information, formula or process that derives independent economic value from not being generally known or readily ascertainable by others that can obtain economic value from its disclosure or use and is the subject of reasonable efforts to maintain its secrecy.

Note that Legend did not discover or disclose the manufacturing system. Instead, Skin Repair is alleging that the characteristics of the collagen it uses in its manufacturing system is the misappropriated trade secret.

Formulas like the collagen mixture at issue can be protected as trade secrets if they are not generally known, have economic value, and are kept secret. Skin Repair uses standard industry practices to keep its raw materials and manufacturing system a secret. Only a few employees seem to know the characteristics of the raw materials. Thus, it is likely that the characteristics of the raw materials are subject to reasonable efforts to maintain their secrecy.

There is also evidence that the method Skin Repair uses to make its products has economic value. For example, consumers prefer to buy Skin Repair's products because of its manufacturing process.

The remaining question is whether the characteristics of the raw materials Skin Repair uses are known. Here, it will be difficult for Skin Repair to show that its raw materials are not generally known or readily ascertainable. It seems to be a well-known fact in the industry that bovine cowhide can be used to make collagen. Further, the pH level is readily ascertainable because Legend's scientists were able to reverse engineer Skin Repair's products to determine the pH level of the collagen. Reverse engineering is a lawful means of acquiring a trade secret.

In sum, the facts that Skin Repair's collagen mixture is economically valuable, and that Skin Repair protects it as a secret weigh in favor of affording the mixture trade secret protection. However, because the characteristics of the collagen mixture was known and the pH level was discovered by Legend through reverse engineering, it is likely not protectable as a trade secret.

■ PROBLEM 10.2 ■

Axis Supply Company ("Axis") manufactures industrial chemicals used by textile cleaning companies. Axis has an extensive customer list. In addition to general customer information such as name and address, the customer list includes details about customers' past orders, customers' order schedules, and their product customization preferences. Axis compiled this customer list over many years and has never made any of it publicly available. Axis' salespeople rely on the customer list to satisfy its most important customers. Axis' salespeople like the customer list because it allows them to provide better customer service than Axis' competitors.

Several copies of Axis' customer list exists throughout its business offices. The receptionist has access to a hard copy of the list at his desk. Also, at least ten salespeople have physical and digital copies of the customer list. The physical copies can be identified by a bright red cover page and the digital copies are accessible to most employees on the company's internal website. It is common practice for salespeople to make copies of the customer list when they leave the building to visit customers. Thus, several salespeople also have a copy of the customer list in their cars or at their home.

Larry, Moe, and Curly have worked as senior managers for Axis since 1995. All Axis employees at the level of senior manager or above sign an agreement with Axis that stipulates that they will not obtain or disclose Axis' confidential information for use by Axis' competitors.

In November of 2000, Larry, Moe, and Curly decide to start their own company. They all agree to turn in their letters of resignation on the same day—January 31, 2001. During the months leading up to their resignation date, Larry, Moe, and Curly continue to work for Axis. While the trio perform their regular duties without interruption during the day, they spend weekends and evenings taking steps to form their new company. The day before they submit their resignation letters, each senior manager makes a copy of a different portion of Axis' customer list. In sum, the trio obtain customer information for about two-thirds of Axis' customers.

Larry, Moe, and Curly begin operating their business, Three Guys Supplies ("Three Guys"), on February 1, 2001. Three Guys competes directly with Axis. Three Guys uses the information from Axis' customer list to solicit business from Axis' customers. By the end of 2001, Three Guys is successful in poaching away 30% of Axis' customers.

Axis sues Larry, Moe, and Curly for trade secret misappropriation.

Discuss.

Analysis

Problem 10.2 involves a departing employee which is a common scenario under which trade secret issues arise. Axis is asserting that its trade secret, a customer list, has been misappropriated by three former employees. However, unlike Problem 10.1, the call of the question is more open-ended. Therefore, it will be important for the student to discuss both whether the subject matter at issue is a trade secret, whether that subject matter has been misappropriated, and appropriate remedies.

A cause of action for the misappropriation of trade secrets requires that the subject matter at issue qualify as a trade secret and be treated as such and that the subject matter be acquired, used or disclosed by a wrongful act.

A trade secret is any information, formula or process that derives independent economic value from not being generally known or readily ascertainable by others that can obtain economic value from its disclosure or use, and is the subject of reasonable efforts to maintain its secrecy. Customers are not trade secrets. However, tangible customer lists have been recognized as trade secrets so long as they are more than basic public information that could be compiled by third parties. Here, Axis' list satisfies that criteria because it includes information such as customers' past orders, customers' order schedules, and their product customization preferences. The customer list has economic value because Axis' salespeople rely on it to make sales. Further, because the information is based on a customer's past orders with Axis, which it has not made public, there is a strong argument that the information in the customer list is not generally known or readily ascertainable.

However, there is a question of whether Axis took reasonable steps to keep the customer list a secret. Several copies of the customer list exist in various formats which can be accessed by anyone at the company. Despite the hardcopies being identified by a red cover, Axis' employees can make copies of the list and transport those copies out of the office. Other than the agreement that upper level Axis employees must sign, there does not seem to be any reasonable security measures in place that will maintain the secrecy of the customer list. Thus, the defendants have a strong argument that the customer list is not a trade secret because Axis failed to take reasonable steps to maintain its secrecy.

Even though it seems clear that a claim for misappropriation would fail because the customer list is not a trade secret, a complete answer should analyze whether, Larry, Moe, and Curly acquired the customer list by a wrongful act. Generally, unlawful disclosure of a trade secret occurs through improper means or by a breach of confidence. Here, there is an argument that Larry, Moe, and Curly acquired Axis' customer list by a breach of confidence. As senior managers, all three signed an agreement no to obtain or disclose Axis' confidential information for use by its competitors. Instead, the trio knowingly made copies of the list on their last day for use at Three Guys which competes directly with Axis. Thus, there is a strong argument that Larry, Moe, and Curly breached an express duty of confidentiality by copying parts of Axis' customer list.

Finally, assuming that a finder of fact determined that the customer list was a trade secret and that the defendants obtained it improperly, Axis would be entitled to damages or injunctive relief. The damages remedy could take the form of Axis' lost profits or Three Guys' profits or some combination of the two. The court could also enjoin Three Guys from using Axis' customer list. Note that this would do little to prevent Three Guys from soliciting business from Axis' customers since basic customer information is not a trade secret.

POINTS TO REMEMBER

- Almost anything can be protected as a trade secret. In certain instances, subject matter may be eligible for both trade secret and patent protection. Remember, however, that a hallmark of trade secret protection is secrecy.

- While a trade secret owner must take reasonable steps to maintain subject matter as a trade secret, absolute secrecy is not required. A trade secret owner can disclose a trade secret to employees or even other companies. However, a trade secret owner must take precautions to prevent public disclosure of its trade secret by third parties.

- Misappropriation of a trade secret requires the defendant to have committed a wrongful act. The defendant must have used improper means or breached a duty of confidence to obtain or disclose the trade secret.

- There are several ways that a third party can obtain a trade secret that are not considered misappropriation. A third party may learn of a trade secret by reverse engineering a commercial product that embodies the trade secret. In addition, a third party may independently discover a trade secret through its own research.

- Remember that the majority of trade secret cases involve departing employees. Do not miss an opportunity on an exam question to discuss how companies use contractual agreements to limit the use and disclosure of trade secrets by departing employees.